KU-487-912

Old English Houses

by the same author

*

THE STORY OF ENGLISH ARCHITECTURE
HISTORICAL ARCHITECTURE
THE RESTORATION OF OLD HOUSES
AN INTRODUCTION TO
ENGLISH MEDIEVAL ARCHITECTURE

OLD ENGLISH HOUSES

by

HUGH BRAUN
F.S.A., F.R.I.B.A.

FABER AND FABER LIMITED

24 Russell Square

London

First published in mcmlxii
by Faber and Faber Limited
24 Russell Square London W.C.1
Printed in Great Britain
by Ebenezer Baylis and Son Limited
The Trinity Press, Worcester, and London
All rights reserved

TO ROLY AND FELIX

Contents

	FOREWORD	*page* 13
I	THE MEDIAEVAL HOUSE	17
II	THE HOME OF THE TUDOR YEOMAN	43
III	ELIZABETHAN AND JACOBEAN STANDARDIZED PLANNING	65
IV	THE LONG HOUSES OF THE SEVENTEENTH CENTURY	84
V	THE GEORGIANS	111
VI	THE NINETEENTH CENTURY	134
	POSTSCRIPT	149
	GLOSSARY	153
	INDEX	159

Illustrations

PLATES

1. Lavenham, Suffolk *facing page* 16
2. Houghton, Huntingdonshire 17
3. Lacock, Wiltshire 32
4. Aldbury, Hertfordshire 33
5. Eling, Hampshire 52
6. Somersby, Lincolnshire 53
7. Grantchester, Cambridgeshire 60
8. Great Bardfield, Essex 61
9. Salford Priors, Warwickshire 68
10. Charmouth, Dorset 69
11. Selworthy, Somerset 76
12. Cropthorne, Worcestershire 77
13. Groombridge, Kent 84
14. Broadchalke, Wiltshire 85
15. Stanton, Gloucestershire 92
16. Broadway, Worcestershire 93
17. Wherwell, Hampshire 100
18. Boscastle, Cornwall 101
19. Milton Abbas, Dorset 108
20. Box Hill, Surrey 109
21. Winterbourne Came, Dorset 128
22. New Forest, Hampshire 129
23. Blackheath, Kent 144
24. Godmanchester, Huntingdonshire 145

The photographs reproduced in plates 6, 15 and 21

are by Reece Winstone, A.I.B.P., A.R.P.S., F.R.S.A.; and in plates 10, 14, 19 *and* 23 *by A. F. Kersting, A.I.B.P., F.R.P.S. All the remaining photographs are by Noel Habgood, F.R.P.S.*

DIAGRAMS

1.	The feudal hall	*page* 24
2.	The early stone-built house	29
3.	The feudal manor house	31
4.	Late-medieval priest's house	34
5.	Tudor manor house	39
6.	Yeomen's houses of the Tudor era	54
7.	Elizabethan/Jacobean standard farmhouse	75
8.	Seventeenth-century 'long house'	78
9.	Rubble-stone farmhouse	80
10.	Wings added to long houses	88
11.	Renaissance manor-farmhouse	95
12.	Georgian house-plan	98
13.	Development of humbler type of farmhouse	104
14.	Plan of Georgian cottage	113
15.	Squaring-up the long house	116
16.	Georgian modifications to the plans of long houses	123
17.	Origin of the L-shaped plan	127

Foreword

Stroll through any one of England's ten thousand villages with a discerning eye upon the buildings gazing back at you. Ignore the colony of council houses, the new parish hall, the occasional modern villa or bungalow. . . . Until, as you reach the village centre, you enter into the heart of England.

It is the same everywhere, with just those differences which remind you where you are. In the wind-swept North or West there will be sturdy walls of rubble stone or smooth cob about you. If you are in the Midlands, or the soft south-eastern counties, it will be warm red brick with here and there a bit of old black timbering for seasoning. The Cotswolds will display to you the dignity and grace of fine-wrought masonry.

There will be smart square houses with panelled sash windows, long raking houses with casement windows, here and there windows piled up into a timbered gable end jettied out over the street. There will be cottage rows with groups of little porches—all different, many flower-covered—framing their entrances.

There will be roofs of tile, great stone slabs, thatch in every stage of decrepitude, with dormer windows peeping through them. Here and there, massive groups of chimneys will thrust above them to tell of cavernous fire-hearths within.

Should your business take you into one of these village homes, you may find yourself beneath a ceiling of oaken timbers, warmed by a blackened fireplace flanked by odd niches and cupboards. You may catch a glimpse of a staircase, narrow and confined, or perhaps enchantingly balustraded.

And as you emerge once more into the village street and glance about you, you can tell yourself that most of this goes back two hundred years and more into English history.

13

Foreword

Which is what the following pages are designed to illustrate.

Most people are interested in finding out the dates at which their houses were founded (which of course may bear no relation to documentary evidence of the house having existed on the same site in some earlier form) and by following their architectural development down the centuries, through various alterations and additions, try to fit them into the fascinating saga which is English history.

There are a number of factors to be considered when trying to date features of a small house in the heart of the English countryside. Broadly speaking, our domestic architecture may be divided into three main periods. The first is the Mediaeval, during which innovations in planning and detailing were distributed fairly smoothly through the medium of masoncraft. After the middle of the eighteenth century, the same service was rendered by the improved transport facilities—road, canal, and railway—of the Industrial Age. During what may be called the Renaissance Era, however—say from 1550 to 1750—a considerable time-lag intervened which greatly affects the successful dating of small houses.

We may classify houses into three main types. First come the great houses of the land—the Hatfields and Blenheims— with which this book is not concerned. Architectural innovations first appear in them and spread so swiftly and smoothly among them that they may be evenly dated. It may take a generation, however, for such novelties to reach our second class of houses, the fine manor and country houses which really provide the backbone of our domestic architecture. And then perhaps another quarter-century or so passes before the farmhouses which are our third and most prolific class begin to benefit from discoveries which first appeared in England fifty years earlier.

There is yet another factor—the regional. The most advanced of these—what we may call the Inner Zone—is the south-east with its sea and river ports offering first contact with the Continent. It may be said to be bounded, very approximately, by a line joining Norwich with Winchester and separating it from an easily distinguishable Midland Zone; finally there is an Outer Zone represented by the North and West. (Scotland had of course its own individual architectural development through Edinburgh.)

Each of these three zones may be said to be separated by approximately a generation when it comes to dating houses, not of the first class, believed to be of the seventeenth century or thereabouts. This regional time-lag has to be added to that concerned with the social classification noted above; thus we may find a farmhouse in, say, Westmorland which is architecturally a century behind the latest style. The same factors apply of course to the dating of alterations and additions to existing buildings.

Unless specifically noted, the dating suggested in the following chapters relates to small houses situated in the south-east or Inner Zone.

The author hopes that his readers will be able to work out for themselves the architectural history of any small house with the aid of the plans in this book.

The earlier of these are set out 'axonometrically' and intend to suggest the building cut off about three feet above the ground.

All the plans are diagrammatic only and illustrate current basic ideas while making no allowance for regional and individual vagaries.

There is no orientation—as there is with a church—affecting domestic planning (though the mediaeval superstition that the plague was carried by the south wind caused builders to eschew south windows). There was generally a 'show front' though this does not mean that it was necessarily architecturally embellished. Naturally there was a 'back side' connected with the offices of service. The principal feature was the main entrance doorway. But whether one turned left or right from it to reach the principal room was entirely a matter for local convenience.

Thus any of the following plans may be 'mirrored' (literally if so desired for comparison with an existing building) by turning end for end——

15

1. A great town house of the days of the Tudor wool boom at Lavenham in Suffolk. The jetty is here utilized as an impressive architectural feature, supported by an elaborately-carved teazle-post at the angle and punctuated by oriel windows.

2. A mid-sixteenth-century house at Houghton in Huntingdonshire which has been modernized at the turn of the century by the insertion of a large chimney-stack between living room and parlour.

CHAPTER I

The Mediaeval House

This is not a book about Architecture. We shall not rouse the echoes in rambling palaces, turreted or pedimented against the sky. We shall pass by cold façades—perhaps with tiers of uncurtained windows gazing out over neglected parks—relics of circumstances which have faded into English history. Neglecting these playgrounds of bygone fashionable architects, amateur and dilettante, we shall turn instead to the achievements of craftsmen-builders whose trade was the making of homes—homes in which even today we may yet enjoy the grace and comfort their labours provided.

Those of us who may be privileged to live in the houses of our ancestors may count ourselves fortunate in feeling about us the walls they built, above us the roofs they raised. Lacking though they may be in many of the fashionable amenities of our day—the labour-saving devices, the functional/decorative fantasies which are the pride of the modern architect—they can yet give us what neither the efficiency nor the frivolity of contemporary architecture can ever in this world supply . . .

The serenity which is the legacy of age—the graciousness which deepens with the patina of history.

In the beginning our rustic forefathers lived in mere lairs, fashioned among dense bushes or in the branches of trees where the claws of forest beasts could not pluck them from sleep. When fire was conquered, man could seize the dens of the ranging beasts and with a fire burning at each cave-mouth prevent their reoccupation by the enemy. Only after the wild sheep and cattle had been tamed to the service of mankind could our ancestors exchange the profession of hunter for that of herdsman and

17   B

follow their flocks from pasture to pasture, building in the lee of bluff or woodland simple shelters of plaited wattle thatched with bracken or heather.

It is to the taming of plants that we may ascribe the beginnings of architecture. The family of the husbandman have no need to pull up sticks and follow their property across the countryside; what they need is a stationary dwelling whence they may supervise the growth and ripening of each season's crop. And once the home has become permanently established there is some encouragement for its owner to improve it.

We think of a house today in terms of its walls and roof; in reality, however, it is only the roof which counts, the walls being merely a luxury added to provide adequate headroom should we wish to pace about the whole of the floor area. If we except those sophisticated dwellings introduced by the imperial Romans during the ten generations or so of their *raj*, it is probably safe to say that it is only about a thousand years or so since the wall-supported roof first appeared in some of the finest houses of our land. Rafter and thatch were what made the early homes of Britain weather-proof.

By 'thatch' is meant any substance which can be laid upon a roof in order to keep out the rain. There are, of course, the normal thatching materials of today such as straw and reed, the technique of laying which was probably unknown to our primitive forefathers. There were also heather, bracken, and turves, as well as ordinary clay reinforced with sticks or the basketwork known as 'wattle'. A specification which suggests itself is clay daubed upon wattle or heather and covered in its turn with another layer of heather. A winter or two would probably consolidate the whole into a reasonably impervious concrete.

It will be noted here at the outset the fundamental necessity in early times for having available *at hand* the materials necessary for home-building: the clay, the moorland heather, the forest bracken, the swamp-willow for wattle. But even where something was lacking there was usually something else to take its place: the clayless areas could perhaps provide a thicker thatch of heather and bracken. And nearly always, in any district where the fields of the husbandman could support his family, there was a natural roofing material to be found in ordinary turf.

Such were the roofs of our primitive ancestors—little hillocks of turf, gay with wild flowers in summer. . . . Watched over by those greater mounds where, in their eternal homes, still sleep the ancient kings of Britain.

The house-thatch had to be carried over the heads of those living beneath it by some system of raftering. It is in devising this that the skill of the house-builder must lie; thus it is the rafter which is the key to the roof and to the home which it covers.

The rafter itself can be only one thing: a wooden pole. But one rafter does not make a roof, nor two or three unless these can be joined together to make a rigid framework upon which thatch can be laid. The simplest way to make such a framework is to lean the rafters together and lash their tops: this in fact was the form of the peasant's roof until much later in our history than we should like to believe. It is not a bad form of construction, for even if the lashing at the head of the framework begins to give way the whole roof may lock together into a sort of dome and may still keep the whole edifice together.

The inconvenience one would have noted when living in such a house would have been one's inability to stand up anywhere in it except in the middle; towards the edges, even squatting on the floor would have involved assuming a folded-up attitude. The extra headroom so desperately needed could be obtained however by excavating the floor of the house, piling up the soil thus obtained round the feet of the rafters and thereby adding something to the thickness of the protecting walling near the floor where it was most needed.

In hard soils, however, where excavation was not possible, a different technique had to be evolved. This was probably due in the first place to the fact that the feet of the poles could not be dug into the earth to prevent their sliding apart and the whole structure collapsing. Soil had therefore to be imported and piled in a ring around the house-site to anchor the feet of the rafters. To keep the soil in position two rings of stones had to be set out to act as inner and outer kerbs. By building these two kerbs first and raising them to form low walls, not only was the problem of the stability of the roof achieved, but also that of headroom. Incidentally the erection of the two stone walls and the filling in between them of a core of earth marks the beginnings of the masonry technique of later days.

It will be realized from the above description of early house-building that the fundamental factor is the wooden pole or rafter. Yet in the tempest-ravaged lands of the West, where no trees could grow, the inhabitants of two thousand years ago were still able to raise a roof over their heads. This part of Britain having had the advantage of occasional contact with the ancient civilizations of the Middle East, some early resident was shown by a venturesome merchant how to construct a dome. Under instruction he gathered lumps of field-stone, set them carefully locked together over a mound of soil provided to act as 'centering', removed the soil—and found he had built a roof. At Bosporthprennis near Penzance one such house, still roofed, may yet be seen.

Not far away is a village consisting of a number of houses built after a fashion also very exotic. The distant homes of those ancient travellers would have been built round court-yards; it is interesting to see how this planning device was imitated by the Cornish builders of Chysauster. Each house is large in area and is surrounded by two stone walls a considerable distance apart, the innermost enclosing a roughly circular courtyard. In the space between the two walls are set out small oval rooms, each of which could be roofed by means of short rafters with their ends embedded in the soil with which the remaining space was filled.

But such excursions as these may have no real bearing on the story of English house-building. Nor may we claim any past assistance in the matter from our Roman masters who erected their timber-framed bungalows—first in cantonments and then on the fertile estates they won from the countryside. While the ruins of some of the Roman public buildings may yet be seen as shapeless snags of brickwork lurking within the perimeters of massive town walls, little save foundations is left of the homes of the Roman colonists, or those of their subjects who may have copied their ways. Save for one feature, the pavements of stone *tesserae* with which they covered the earthen floors of their dwellings. Though most of these were simple enough, some were wrought into patterns and even into pictorial designs; it is only by the occasional emergence from beneath the soil of one of these lovely carpets that we may be reminded of the vanished homes—colonial, ephemeral—of the England the Romans knew.

But the round huts—or oval, for the roofing system could be stretched to allow of a more conveniently shaped floor area— remained as the homes of our forefathers in those days of fifteen hundred years ago. There were no professional house-builders; if a man wanted a house he had to build it himself after the simple fashion he could see all about him.

Some houses may have been larger than others. The palace of a tribal chieftain probably comprised a group of houses (some of which may have been joined together), for even if some despot had the means of enforcing a subject to build a house for him the builder would have had to rely on the standard amateur technique. The Roman system of building frames of squared timbers was dependent upon the existence of well-fashioned tools and it seems doubtful whether the craft of house-carpenter was able to survive the break-up of the colony and the collapse of its administration.

But with the arrival of Anglo-Saxon invaders the house-carpenter or 'wright' appears in full strength. Every settlement, manor or township seems to have been equipped with some-one who knew how to square logs and build with them. The development of the pit-saw, with one man standing on the log pulling up the blade while the 'underdog' stood in the pit in a shower of sawdust and pulled it down, encouraged the development of the science of house-building as we know it today. For squared balks can be joinered together to produce a construction of a rigidity unattainable if round poles tied together are used. So the trade of sawyer became of primary importance in the life of the Anglo-Saxon community, for soon he was learning the use of the chisel and auger, the making of mortices and tenons, and the pinning of joints with strong wooden pegs cut wherever possible from heartwood. At last, as fully-fledged 'wright', he became the accredited house-builder of the English township.

As a tradesman the wright had, of course, to be paid for his skill; thus his services could only be employed for building the house of a man of property.

There is yet much research to be undertaken before we can

be sure of the form of the Anglo-Saxon 'hall' but there are certain features of it which have come down to us which help us to conjecture something of the principles upon which the wright worked. The intention was certainly to produce a building on a rectangular plan in place of the inconvenient conical hut. The builder achieved this by standing four posts upon two horizontal ground-sills and carrying across them four beams which in their turn supported the middles of the rafters as they rose from the ground to meet at the summit of a pyramidal structure covered with thatch of some description. Later the rafters were covered with rough planking, produced as a by-product of the squaring of the logs, and, as a crowning refinement, finished with wooden 'thatch-tile' or shingles made from the waste timber. The timber was, of course, the local oak, only straight trees being used and everything being of impressively massive scantling.

Doorways would be simply openings left in the walling and closed with simple doors of planking, the openings of windows being similarly closed with shutters—those pathetic *fenestres* of which we are told the English peasants tried to make a shield wall against the invader at Hastings long ago.[1] Even in the absence of glazing it should have been quite possible to keep a house weathertight by opening the shutters on the leeward side only.

The principal contribution of the Anglo-Saxons to the timber-building craft in this country was undoubtedly their introduction of the 'ground-sill'. Prior to this the native builders would have planted the poles of their houses in the earth; a bad practice as water would rise up the end-grain of the timber to rot it where it emerges from the ground. It may have been Anglo-Saxon shipwrights who first taught the housewrights how to step a mast on a keel and so provide a sound foundation for the posts of a house. Certainly from this time onwards the ground-sill remains as the basis for all timber house construction.

It will be noticed that such posts were used to carry roof timbers and were not intended to form part of the framing of walls. Indeed, had the feet of the rafters been freed from their safe anchorage in the earth the whole structure would have collapsed. By the same token there were no gables or gable

1 See L. F. Salzman *Building in England* p. 256

ends, for no one could have built a wall high enough to fill them.

A true wall—as opposed to a timber screen or partition—is of stone set in mortar. The stone would at first have been field stone picked up from moor or ploughland; later it was ragstone dug out of a quarry. The mortar would at first have been just clay in which each rough stone was set to build up a wall of more or less uniform thickness. Later the larger stones could be trimmed to squareness and set to form neater faces on either side of the wall with a core of clay and smaller stones between them.

Anyone can build a length of stone wall in this fashion. It is only when he needs to change direction that he is in difficulties over building an angle which will not fall down. The first English stone-builders went to great lengths to hack from old Roman ruins the bricks with which they could fashion the angles of their rough rubble walls. Bit by bit, however, they were taught—probably through the efforts of visiting Benedictine monks—how to quarry and dress true freestone until they could work it into blocks with which to make the angles of their rubble buildings secure.

Such blocks had to be set in a better mortar than clay. The English builders had thus to learn also the art of burning limestone to make lime, mixing this with sand to make a sound mortar which would not be affected by the scouring of the rain.

The first English stone quarries were probably those of the Bath region discovered and opened at the beginning of the eighth century by Byzantine craftsmen imported by St. Aldhelm. These men, who would also have burnt the lime and laid the stone in St. Aldhelm's churches, were probably able to train apprentices from the local folk; these in their turn spreading the knowledge gained throughout the freestone belt which passes with the Cotswolds towards Northamptonshire and so into Yorkshire. In this way was founded in England the trade of masoncraft.

But during the centuries which followed, it was the Church which reaped where undoubtedly it had sown, commandeering the whole of the mason-craft and setting it to the building of churches and monasteries. So the wrights still held the whole of the house-building trade in their hands. And being called in to construct the roofs of stone-walled churches, they had to learn how to tie together the feet of rafters so that the whole assembly would not spread and collapse. Thus they were constructing roofs having two planes meeting together along the axis of the building at a 'ridge'—an innovation which enabled them to extend their pyramidal halls by adding another pair of posts, re-erecting the removed portion of the roof at the new end, and filling up the centre portion with one of the new ridged

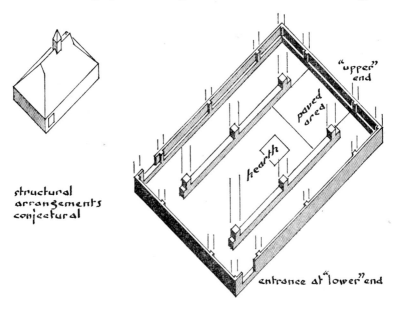

Fig. 1. *The feudal hall—one of the units which combine to form the mediaeval manor house*

roofs. There was, of course, no possibility of having a gable-end as in a church for there were no masons available to build such a lofty feature. But the hall was now definitely provided with an axis; from being a mere tent it could now accommodate if required not only the owner and his family but also the teams of plough-oxen, valuable animals far removed in status from the half-wild cattle of earlier times. (Fig. 1).

The building trade being now firmly established, contract formalities between owner and builder had to be considered and a system of measurement had to be devised.

Mediaeval mensuration was a simple matter. Sixteen men were collected in the church porch one Sunday morning and by placing their right feet one behind the other made to set out the length of the village pole. This module, representing stall-room for a yoke of four plough-oxen, became the basis for measuring the furlong—the length of the furrow—and from this the mile. Used for square measure it produced the rood and acre. (Sixteen-foot poles tipped with steel were carried by the pikemen of Edgehill.)

A cord or thong of pole length, twice folded, gave the cord or yard (still used as a measure for firewood). Further sub-division of the pole by means of folded cords, checked by trial and error, gave the smallest unit in use, the foot itself.

During the later Middle Ages the continental clothiers introduced the cloth-yard—the distance between the finger-tips and the end of the nose with the head turned away. This yard, being in more general use than the Anglo-Saxon yard, eventu-ally took its place; the pole had then to be divided into the five-and-a-half yards of the present day, with corresponding complications of the furlong, mile, and acre (to say nothing of surveyors' chains and cricket pitches).

The sixteen-foot pole is encountered everywhere in the plans of mediaeval domestic buildings. Small buildings are often a pole wide and two in length; the halls of manor houses two poles in span and four pole-width bays in length.

Should anyone be interested in trying to work out the metro-logy of an old house, it is of interest to find that the primary dimension is its internal span—that is to say, the distance to be covered by the length of beam available. The length of the building, however, was usually measured overall—that is to say, externally. At the beginning of the seventeenth century the size of the minimum house was given as sixteen feet by thirty; this is actually one pole by two as the gable walls are allowed for in the two-poles' length.

The rather cumbersome sixteen-foot bay module was often abandoned by the builders of the well-constructed framed buildings of the Tudor period in favour of a three-yard module of twelve feet which besides being more manageable was also capable of being used in connection with the more up-to-date cloth yard of three feet. This twelve-foot module was adopted as standard by the Elizabethan surveyors when they were called upon to sketch out plans of new houses for their clients.

What a pity it is that the duodecimal system, so convenient for practical purposes, is now in process of being abandoned in favour of the unmanageable decimal system which takes us back to a primitive age which could see no further than the ends of its ten fingers! If the mathematicians must inflict a metric system upon us why cannot they have the courage to devise two new cyphers so that their system may be convenient in practice as well as on paper.

By the tenth century England had become a country of fine buildings. The wooden halls of her people had no rivals in western Europe; her masons had been launched by the Church upon a building programme which at the close of the following century was to produce in England the mightiest buildings in the whole world.

Not only were great churches being built. By the eleventh century the monastic houses were beginning to provide their monks with accommodation of a kind never before seen in this country. Of enormous size, and built, of course, in masonry, the monastic houses had lofty stone walls and moreover possessed a completely revolutionary feature—they had upper floors. In order to appreciate the reasons for this remarkable refinement —no English noble, perhaps even the King himself, could boast he slept above ground level—it is necessary to stray for a space into the sphere of historical architecture.

Our monumental—as opposed to our native—architecture derives from the regions which at this time formed the eastern part of the Byzantine Empire. Byzantine building technique was closely allied to that of the Middle East, a region which provided its houses with flat roofs, pleasant to live on during fine weather. The Byzantine house thus differed from the Roman's bungalow type of residence in favouring a *piano nobile*, an upper floor which provided the best of the living accommodation raised above the ground. Thus whereas the Roman, colonnades and mosaic floors notwithstanding, had still been living, in primitive fashion, 'on the ground', the Byzantines moved upwards and left their ground storeys to their animals or used them as storerooms.

The Byzantine type of dwelling first appears in this country, as might have been expected, in monumental form. The eleventh-century keep towers of Norman castles not only have their principal rooms on the first floor but are entered at that level, the storage space at ground level being accessible only by a stair from above.

The introduction of the *piano nobile* into English domestic architecture was only partially effected at this time. During the daytime, life in the western house went on as before. But one feature of the Byzantine way of life became firmly established and has remained a part of English custom to the present day. The Englishman likes to go upstairs to bed. Only our colonies have abandoned this practice and gone back to the primitive 'bungalow'.

At the beginning of the second millennium most of Europe, including Anglo-Saxon England, was under the cultural influence of the Byzantines, imitating them whenever local conditions permitted. But whereas the English layman was debarred from building a two-storied house through lack of masons, the Church, having the monopoly, was able to house its monks in accordance with the best conditions known to the age.

By the beginning of the twelfth century the great churches were being completed. But as mid-century drew near the country was plunged into the terrible years of the Anarchy —when it was said that 'God and His Saints slept'—and the arts of building had perforce to be neglected. Then the long reign of Henry II saw a spate of castle-building which, although it absorbed much of the building potential of the country, laid the foundations of a peaceful and united England.

The twelfth century was the era of the Crusades, when our rude forefathers sallied forth, from homes which today would be classed as barns or stables, to do battle with the most highly civilized people in the world living amidst luxury and culture in vast palaces exquisitely decorated and equipped with all the appurtenances of delight. It is probably due to our contact with the Moslems that we owe our possession of some of the most remarkable buildings in the world, the noble keep-towers which lift their lofty chambers on the summits of castle mounds. Known only in those districts which formed part of the Norman empire they are probably derived from Moslem palace towers encountered in that region of their conquests which lay in what is now Tunisia.

While no discussion of English homes may dare to omit some reference to these princely structures, they do however lie somewhat outside the scope of the present book, the aim of which is to deal with the kind of house which may be inhabited today. And there are certainly quite a number of occupied houses in this country of which there are portions dating back to the very end of the twelfth century, when the great churches and the great towers were finished at last and private personages were at last able to build for themselves houses of stone.

These early stone houses—'King John's houses' they are often called—were very humble little structures. They are never more than twenty feet wide internally and less than twice that in length. The ground floor was used for keeping the owner's valuables—in the days before banks this would really represent all his movable wealth—while on the upper floor he and his family lived in just the single room, perhaps divided up by hangings or wooden screens. The floor, which was known as the 'solar'—pronounced *soller*—was often of wood but this was not very suited to the primitive customs of the age so wherever possible a stone floor ('stone solar') was provided, carried by vaulting rising from two or three sturdy stone columns. The entrance was by ladder or steps to a door on the first floor from which an internal stair led down to the thief-proof ground floor. The living-room had a fireplace and, generally, a latrine, with a square drain, built out in a small buttress. The ground-floor windows were kept very narrow but on the *piano nobile* there were pretty double windows with slender central shafts, closed by wooden shutters. Sometimes a diminutive chapel was built out from the house. (Fig. 2).

For the most part these little 'King John's houses' represent the homes of private personages. They may be country houses —in which case they were probably originally attached to a timber hall—or the home of the castellan of some walled stronghold. Many, however, were the town houses of wealthy merchants, in which case the ground floor was usually entered direct from the street and formed a shop or workroom. Probably the best-known group of twelfth-century town houses is that in the ancient city of Lincoln believed to have been built by Jewish merchants towards the end of the century.

This type of stone-built town house continued in use throughout the thirteenth century and many of our old towns can still show examples. Their vaulted ground floors have generally by

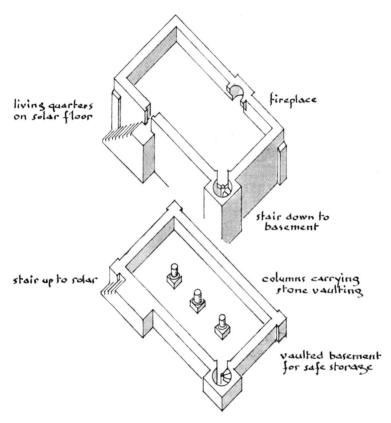

living quarters on solar floor

fireplace

stair down to basement

stair up to solar

columns carrying stone vaulting

vaulted basement for safe storage

Fig. 2. The other unit making up the English manor-house—the stone-built Byzantine house ('King John's house'). A wooden floor carried on posts is sometimes used in place of columns and vaulting

now become reduced in level through the rising of the streets, and now appear as cellars buried deep below shops and inn-rooms.

Some of these little houses belonged to religious foundations.

The long monastic house attached to a transept—usually the southern—of the great church is too well known for it to be necessary to dwell upon these impressive structures, some portions of which may have survived the assaults of the Dissolution to become incorporated within houses inhabited today. What is more likely, however, is that the sole surviving relic of a great monastery may be the little house which once formed the private residence of its abbot and was preserved when all else was destroyed to be the nucleus of a home for the new owner of the property. For many a twelfth-century abbot built for himself a small house projecting from the buildings on the western side of the cloister, near the church and overlooking the passage which led into the cloister from the outside world. Cistercian abbots, who were supposed to sleep in the communal dormitory, built their own houses adjoining this and thus on the opposite side of the cloister from those of their Benedictine colleagues. To this brief summary of clerical private residences may be added those constructed by twelfth-century bishops adjoining their cathedrals.

There are still a number of 'King John's houses' scattered through the countryside. Perhaps the most interesting of all is that in the abbey town of Romsey; its chamber once sheltered nobles of the court of Edward I who amused themselves by scratching on its plastered walls their coats of arms and mottoes together with a most realistic portrait of the king wearing his crown.

These little two-storied houses must have seemed very exotic to the Englishman of the turbulent days of King John. The poor man still lived in his lowly thatched hovel, the townsman in a sort of shed set endwise to the street and separated from its neighbours—according to King Henry II's wise fire-precaution bylaws—by walls of rough stone carrying the rafter-feet of the houses on either side of it.

The traditional English upper-class home was still the spacious barn-like hall. Though often still keeping to its great oaken posts, the hall of the days of King John had sometimes profited by the release of the masons to replace its primitive-looking sloping ends by lofty gable-walls between which the roof-tree spread from end to end of the building. Well-braced internal timbering could now allow the roof to be raised upon low side walls. Some of the finer halls of the day replaced their timber posts with stone arcades carried upon sturdy columns, after the fashion of the naves of the new parish churches which were at the time being built.

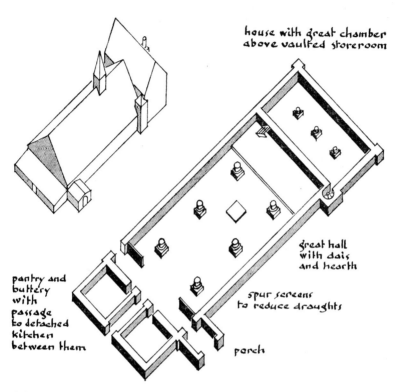

Fig. 3. The two units combined in the twelfth century to form the feudal manor house

Yet the low sprawling mass of the domestic hall could still not compete in dignity of elevation with the great halls or refectories of the monasteries.

Originally nothing more than a combined byre and barn, with the family living at one end and the oxen stalled along the sides and facing towards a narrow passage leading from the door to the living-space, the great hall of the twelfth century had become a fine apartment from which the animals had been

31

ejected to give space for storage and the accommodation of house-servants. Close to the 'upper' end was now a permanent fire-hearth to warm the building, the cooking fire outside the original entrance being housed in a proper kitchen joined to the hall by a covered way. Flanking this approach were two stores —pantry for bread, buttery for drink—having service hatches opening into the hall. (Fig. 3).

A service-area was kept clear across the end of the hall having at either end of it a door, one of which became the main entrance. To keep away draughts short 'spurs' or boarded screens were set against the walls of the hall; later a movable central screen was added, and eventually the whole feature became a permanent partition with two doors left in it for service. At the upper end of the hall was soon to be a paved space—the 'dais'—upon which the family could live above the mess which littered the earth floor—or 'marsh'—of the great apartment.

Few of these barn-like structures remain today. Focus of the life of the mediaeval manor, the great hall was the architectural monument to the feudal system and with its decay declined also. Its importance lies, however, in the fact that it was to continue to survive as the nucleus of the great house of the later Middle Ages.

There are still some twelfth-century halls remaining in part; perhaps other remains are yet to be extricated from among a jumble of later additions. Remains of their timber posts may be concealed within the walling, as at the bishop's palace at Farnham in Surrey where one may open a small cupboard and find an oaken capital that was carved nearly eight centuries ago. Much of the twelfth-century roof—also carved with ornament— remains above the ceiling of the bishop's hall at Hereford. But these are treasures indeed; there must be little walling, and even less timberwork, surviving today in English homes which may be dated with any assurance to the days of the Crusades. And at that time only the very finest domestic halls were stone-built; such masonry skill as might be obtainable was usually employed in building the much smaller houses.

The royal palace of the twelfth century consisted of a straggle of 'King John's houses' grouped about the area focused upon the king's hall. The beginnings of a great house are seen when one such house becomes directly attached to the 'upper' end of the hall itself, providing a private residence in which the family could sleep, descending to the dais at meal-times and for public conference. (Fig. 3). Henceforth these two structures, the hall and the house, are always to be met with in what may be called the mediaeval 'great house'. And it is of interest to remember that long after an ancient wooden hall has rotted or burned away to oblivion, the two-storied stone house beside it may remain today as the nucleus of a country mansion. There are probably still mutilated examples of 'King John's houses' to be disinterred from amidst centuries of subsequent accretions which have long concealed their existence.

Late thirteenth-century bishops, who with their colleagues the abbots had prior access to the architectural skill of the country, built palaces for themselves on a more sophisticated plan. They provided a wide stone hall after the fashion of the monastic refectories but even more elaborate architecturally. One bay of the building was divided into two stories having the bishop's 'great chamber' set above the pair of storerooms, pantry and buttery, at the *lower* end of the hall.

The monopoly of masoncraft was not limited to the senior ranks of the clergy. The parish priest often had a house built for him, in which case it was usually a diminutive version of the bishop's palace with a tiny hall or living-room and a chamber over two store-rooms. (Fig. 4). A number of mediaeval priests' houses remain, stone-built and excellently finished in the best ecclesiastical style.

The hall was as it were the public assembly place of the whole household, not in any sense a private home—though doubtless a corner of it might have provided some humble servant of a great household with the only home he knew—and certainly no dwelling place for women and young children. And while these could live in comparative peace and privacy in the great chamber on the upper storey of the adjoining house, the problem eventually arose of what to do with anyone My Lord might bring home to stay for the night. In palatial houses, provision for the accommodation of visiting notables became a necessity; thus in the great royal palaces of the end of the twelfth century the relatives of the king and the principal officers of state each had a two-storied 'King John's house'

33   C

provided somewhere within the wall enclosing the straggling huddle of structures filling the palace area.

In the small stone houses of the thirteenth century, the upper floor was the storey which mattered. The whole of the living accommodation was provided on it. The lower storey could be used, as in the private houses, as a private store connected with the storey above by stair or ladder. Or it could be used separately from the chamber floor and entered from a doorway or doorways at ground level: this became the practice soon after the end of the twelfth century. Sometimes it was used as a stable—perhaps for the animal belonging to the occupant of the *piano nobile*—in which case the external doorway is made wider than usual.

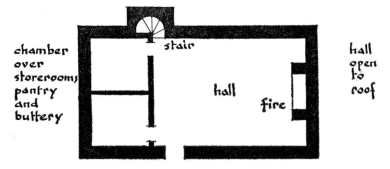

Fig. 4. Type of late-mediaeval priest's house

A century later, during the heyday of the great castles of the fourteenth century, ranges of apartments known as 'lodgings' were built to provide rooms for garrison and visitors. Such lodgings would often be built against the interior face of a castle wall, to extend the accommodation provided by the wall-towers with which all such structures were now equipped. Ordinary unfortified houses might have a range of lodgings set out as a wing at right-angles to the main structure containing the great hall. The canons of cathedrals were housed in a range of lodgings erected as an isolated building within the close; its upper floor—the earthen ground floors of the period were still, of course, unfit for polite occupation—being divided by solid partitions into a number of chambers. (Thus appears in English architecture for the first time the stone wall employed not to

34

carry a roof but as a partition only.) Each lodging would have to have a fireplace similar to that in the chamber of a 'King John's house'—we begin to find houses with more than one chimney stack.

We are beginning to arrive at the complete picture of a late-mediaeval 'great' house—the lofty hall, the great chamber raised high beside it, the ranges of guest chambers, the whole covered by high-pitched roofs flanked here and there by massive chimneys. And, of course, the great house itself forming the central nucleus of a huddle of outbuildings of all descriptions, domestic offices and even farm buildings, some of the lesser structures of rough rubble stone or merely timber shacks.

The palaces of the mediaeval bishops illustrate the highest degree of building excellence. Their walling is perhaps of dressed masonry, having two beautifully-finished skins of stone filled with a core of chippings mixed with mortar instead of the rough rubble walling of the ordinary private builder. The openings are framed in moulded stonework and there are large traceried windows filled with glass.

Such buildings as these would be well beyond the means of everyone save the very richest in the land. What might be termed the 'upper middle class' would have to make do with rubble stone laid by a local waller who would have to call in a skilled mason when it came to building the corners and framing the openings.

But by far the majority of the buildings of the Middle Ages —even if one excepts the peasants' hovels—were still being raised by the village carpenters or 'wrights'. These had by now improved their technique to a stage when they were capable of building houses with their roofs raised upon walls. It has been explained that the difficulty which had to be overcome was how to lift the rafter-feet from their anchorage in the ground without their sliding away and the roof collapsing. As this sliding movement caused the 'ridge' of the roof to subside, the problem resolved itself in finding some means of supporting the roof-tree independently of the rafters. By the middle of the twelfth century this had been done.

In many an English village today we may still see cottages displaying in their gable ends pairs of those massive straddled timbers known as 'crucks' which carry the ends of the roof-tree against which the ends of the rafters rest. At first straight beams were used, but as houses grew in length—as in the process of expanding a square house towards the proportions of a hall—it was found that curved timbers caused less obstruction within the building. Henceforth the selection of curved trees for 'crucks' became a factor in the operations of the wrights (3).

It was, of course, the prerogative of those who could afford to employ the house-wright with his supply of pit-sawn timber to raise houses of this sophistication. Today we may call them 'cottages' but they were built as houses for farmers and small-holders; the cottages of their day were but hovels—a Tudor writer describes them as being 'built of elder poles at every lane end'. Froissart comments on the indifference of cottagers whose poor homes were destroyed during warfare, saying 'with three or four poles shortly they would make again their houses'.

Proper walling—even if based upon timber framing—was for those days an expensive luxury to provide. Timber framing enabled the panels to be filled with wattle daubed with a mud plaster; in the absence of such framing it would be necessary to build a solid wall—of considerable thickness in order that it might stand up at all—right up from the ground.

It has been noted that a masonry wall is formed of three components—two outer skins with a core between. If at any time a stone building should become deserted the first thing that would happen to it would be that someone would begin to try to detach from its walling the valuable skins of freestone. If the walling were well-built, the core might still remain sound and standing after its confining skins had been removed.

This discovery may have led to the invention of a new technique in building—that of concrete construction. There was no need to have freestone skins at all; a core could be cast between a 'shuttering' of boards so that when these were removed a concrete wall would remain standing. While such building methods were never employed in first-class work, they proved invaluable for those who wanted to build cheaply in imitation of stone. The material used was mud-concrete or 'cob'. This substance varies considerably with the various regions in which it was employed but can form a very hard concrete of considerable durability; plastered with mud plaster, renewed as it is scoured away, a cob wall will last for ever.

Such mud-concrete construction was employed by the builders of the great palaces of Islam at a period when we in this country were living in barns. Very probably its use was developed in this country following the experiences of Crusaders in the highly-civilized lands of the Middle East.

Cob was still being used in village building well into the last century. But the principal contributor to village architecture has always been the wright or carpenter. Often the whole structure from foundations to ridge was the product of his hands.

In the case of a large stone building, the most important contribution of the carpenter was the system of rafters carrying its roof of thatch, shingles, tiles, or whatever might be the selected covering. Timbers of considerable length were required for the steep roofs of mediaeval times, and they had to be properly squared up by the pit-saw. It was a common mark of royal esteem for the king to present to a noble a set of rafters cut from the royal forests. These were always given in pairs or 'couples', to be 'halved' and pegged together at the apex and set over the building at intervals of a foot or so. The 'couple', in official French, was known as a *chevron*, and this symbol of two lines meeting at an angle became one of the 'charges' of heraldry. The British Army still uses the symbol, curiously inverted, to denote the non-commissioned ranks.

These tall couples were raised side by side across the building with their feet resting on the timber 'wall-plate' and their tops pegged together. Each couple was strengthened near its apex by a short transverse timber known as a 'collar'. These roofs were very unscientific in construction as there was nothing to keep the feet from spreading. As the angle of pitch was lowered with the passing of the mediaeval era, the increased pressure on the walls threatened to overturn these, necessitating the addition of buttresses to stiffen them.

It will now be seen that during the later Middle Ages there were three main classes of domestic buildings. Lowest in the scale were the home-made huts of the peasantry; here and there in towns and villages were the middle-class homes, either built by the village carpenter or two-storied structures raised by semi-skilled rubble-wallers relying upon highly-trained crafts-men for the masonry 'dressings'. The third class is that of the manor house of a great landowner.

The nucleus of a great house was, of course, the hall with its paved 'dais' at the upper end, and the offices reaching away opposite, beyond the hall doors. By the thirteenth century the hall would have been provided with a two-storied stone house built on to it behind the dais. The attachment of these two very dissimilar structures was quite haphazard and—apart from those episcopal experiments noted above—each great house preserved its own independence and developed along its own lines.

The aisled form of hall with lines of posts or columns supporting its wide roof gradually gave place to the simpler unobstructed plan. The last great stone-built aisled halls were raised during the thirteenth century in castles and bishops' palaces, while as masonry usurped the place of timber until only the halls of the less-favoured manor houses continued to employ the latter material, the old form of post-construction went out of use altogether in favour of the simple unobstructed apartment.

It is clear that the ambition of the mediaeval nobleman was to own a structure which could compete in magnificence with the refectory halls of the monasteries with their great height, unencumbered interiors very different from the sprawling barn-like appearance of the domestic hall, and imposing cliffs of lofty walling fashioned in smooth freestone and pierced by brilliant windows. This is indeed the trend towards which the halls of the mediaeval houses strove, indeed surpassing in the end the achievements of their monastic rivals. (Fig. 5). For their part the abbots began to build private halls for their own advertisement, smaller perhaps than the hall of the manor house but making full use of the architectural services for ever at the disposal of the Church.

It is, of course, to the mediaeval Church that we owe the training of the country's corps of masons who through the generations were able ever to improve their art in order to provide English architecture with all the enchanting features of the Gothic era. Especially in the dressing of window openings do we find this skill displayed, first with the narrow slit, then the double window with its central shaft—popular throughout the Byzantine world which gave to us the 'King John's houses'. At last with the coming of the fourteenth century we find proper glazed windows divided up by stone mullions branching in the window-head into traceried patterns.

At this time also we find greater use being made of the mineral resources of the country, the steep old shingled roofs gradually giving place to low-pitch roofs covered with lead sheets and concealed behind a parapet. Instead of overhanging

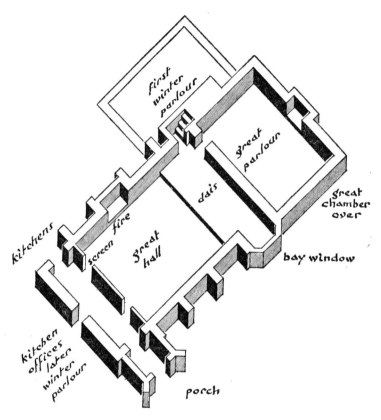

Fig. 5. Plan of a Tudor manor house

eaves we find the summits of the high walls crenellated castle-fashion and punctuated with pinnacles weighting the buttresses by which the thrust of the broad roof was countered.

The principal feature of the hall at this time was its porch. At first merely a protection, partly to keep draught away from the interior of the building and partly as a shelter for persons awaiting an audience, the hall porch begins to expand in

39

magnificence throughout the mediaeval era until it eventually becomes a lofty tower, richly ornamented and vying in splendour with that of the parish church.

The outward manifestation of feudalism, the great hall of the Middle Ages, was embellished as became the principal architectural monument of the *noblesse*. Attention was drawn to the seat of the *seigneur* by the enlargement of the window which lit the dais; this magnificent example of domestic fenestration expanded until it burst forth into the stately bay window which is perhaps the most striking feature of English domestic architecture and remains to this day a favourite feature of the humblest home.

Provision having been made for feudal hospitality, that other factor in our domestic architecture which plays such a large part in house development is aversion to sleeping on the ground floor. This unconscious tribute to our debt to Byzantine civilization may be seen in the homes of the Middle Ages. The way towards this attainment was opened when the stone houses of King John's day first came upon the scene; thenceforth the upper 'chamber' became the feature of every gentleman's house. The way up to the solar was still by a perilous outside stair, even after house and hall had become united—for beneath one's chamber floor was the secret storeroom in which one's worldly possessions were heaped. The next stage in the development of the house was to be achieved as soon as a house-owner could be relieved from the fear that his treasure stood in danger of ravishment.

The house attached to the upper end of a feudal hall, in which the indoor servants of the manor slept during the hours of darkness, being more secure than the isolated examples scattered throughout the lonely countryside, it was sometimes found possible to dispense with the practice of entering the ground floor from the chamber over and making instead a doorway leading out of the hall, at the back of the dais. The next stage was to alter the character of the lower apartment by ejecting the stores and treasure and converting it into a private room for the family: a quiet place for conversation called in Norman-French 'parlour', in Anglo-Saxon speech a stronghold of privacy, *burh* or 'bower'. (Fig. 5).

During the mediaeval era the culture of Islam had steadily

40

been penetrating Europe from Morocco through Spain. The Moorish house had a flat roof carried by large beams which were generally ornamented on their undersides with carving. While our climate made the high roof with its exposed timbering the only covering suitable for an English house, the existence of an upper floor enabled the lower storey to be more warmly ceiled. The old massive stone pillars and the heavy vaulting which covered the obsolete treasury are dispensed with; the beams which support a timber 'solar' can be carved to form an ornamental ceiling to the parlour thus provided.

Throughout the story of English homes the parlour remains as the principal ground-floor room of the house, having above it the principal bedchamber. These two words, chamber and parlour, have only recently passed out of English speech; the hall, which has survived, has only been retained for the reason that into it still leads the entrance doorway, or from it still rises the chamber stair.

While it is not the purpose of this book to consider the greater houses of our country—except in so far as portions of them may yet be retained in lesser houses occupied at this day —it is necessary to appreciate the fundamental nature of the mediaeval manor house, as from it is descended the middle-class home of the Tudor period from which our own houses derive. To recapitulate, therefore, the large house of mediaeval days consisted of a spacious hall having at one end of it a two-storied house with chamber above and parlour beneath. It will be seen in the next chapter how the village wrights adapted this conception to their own idiom while translating finely-dressed masonry into terms of that sturdy oaken framing which so delights us today.

The joisted upper floor or 'solar' being the height of domestic comfort during the Middle Ages, it may be wondered what means of access existed to it. In many cases a ladder was probably the only stair. But in stone buildings a semicircular excrescence bulging out of the wall where hall and house joined, contained a flight of very high wedge-shaped steps forming a rustic imitation of the stone spirals in the turrets of great houses and churches. The ascent from floor to floor having perforce to be achieved in the course of a single semicircle, these fan-shaped stairs were called 'caracoles' in recognition of the wheeling turn the user made when climbing them. Their steps, which were of necessity very high indeed, were often solid wooden balks used in the same fashion as stone.

The joinered timber stairs of today did not appear until the Elizabethan era and even then only in fine houses. In the less sophisticated West and North of England precipitous caracoles continued to be built throughout the seventeenth century.

It will be seen from the foregoing pages that there are very few small *mediaeval* houses—or 'cottages'—remaining in England, and that these are nearly all fragments of one-time large establishments—castles, monasteries, manor houses—of which the greater part has disappeared. Many of these mediaeval rookeries had in their day surprisingly efficient sanitary systems for the disposal of sewage; all monasteries for example had their main drain running eastwards from the monastic house itself.

In those days there were no drain-pipes. Drains were large tunnels built up in stone and roofed over with vaulting. In order that they might be kept clean they were generally large enough for a man to pass along them. These—alas—are the 'secret passages' of romance!

CHAPTER II

The Home of the Tudor Yeoman

———————— ✸ ————————

Revisited today, the English countryside of, say, the fourteenth century would have seemed squalid indeed. Villages of hovels huddled round stone churches and manor houses little better than barns. Shack-lined alleys of tiny towns with still more stone churches packed into their compass. Here and there about the countryside the vast piles of masonry which were the monasteries; alternating with these the gaunt curtains of the castles. On one hand castles and abbeys—on the other hovels and barns. The two halves of England would have been very clearly defined.

But between the two one could have detected an embryo middle class represented by the merchants in the towns and by the holders of some of the poorer or less-favoured manors. It is to this for the moment inconsiderable section of the community to which we must turn in order to follow the growth of the English house, the development of which depended upon the emergence of a class of people which, although not wealthy, could nevertheless share with the highest in the land the services of the *professional builder*. As long as there were just powerful nobles and impotent peasantry this could not be effected; only by recruitment to a middle class could the popular share be won.

The first serious shock to the economic system which formed the basis of mediaeval England came in 1349 with the outbreak of plague in the port of Melcombe Regis in Dorset. For some reason the epidemic took such a hold that the whole of England was swept by the scourge with the result that something like half the population died. There were not enough living to bury

43

the dead. Throughout the countryside the cattle roamed at will amongst rotting crops.

When at last the surviving landowners tried to restore the situation they found that the labour shortage had encouraged the peasantry to hawk their services around the countryside, seeking the highest bidder. A law was passed prohibiting the peasant from leaving his village but Hodge had experienced the virtual breakdown of government during the plague and had tasted many of the fruits of independence. The result was the Peasants' Revolt, by which the rural labourers demonstrated to their employers that Jack could be as good as his master.

The landowners, realizing that agriculture could not be carried on in such circumstances, converted their arable to pasture and took to grazing sheep. The sheep prospered to an extent undreamed-of. No wars—such as plagued the Continent —caused any notable depredations among the flocks. In this fashion were the foundations of Tudor England laid—even to-day the English Chancellor sits upon a Woolsack.

A few of the rebellious labourers got jobs as shepherds. The remainder starved among the ruins of wretched hovels in plague-stricken townships.

> *Poor folk for bread to cry and weep*
> *Towns pulled down to pasture sheep.*

The landowners waxed enormously rich as they 'rode the sheep's back'. Golden fleeces brought riches to expanding Tudor towns. Fleeces travelled abroad and brought riches back to England. Instead of the old habit of exchanging blows, England and the Continent exchanged sheep for scholarship. Englishmen of the upper classes wore magnificent clothes and began to learn the art of living gracefully.

Many of the sheep-farmers had been men who, under the old régime, had been the owners of petty manors driving their peasants to work in order to scratch a living; now they were sitting back and drawing large incomes from a few hundred sheep tended by some shepherds costing in wages a fraction of the wealth they tended. These new-rich sheep-farmers were beginning to form a new social stratum, a genuine middle class between the hereditary noble and the peasantry. Whereas they had in mediaeval days existed as poor relations to the holders of rich manors, the sheep had brought them riches of their own.

> *I thank my God*
> *And ever shall*
> *It was the sheep*
> *That paid for all.*

This new middle class—the 'yeomen' as they may be called—soon became important customers to the building trade. It was now possible for this section of the community to begin to build for itself houses which, although an enormous advance in comfort upon the hovels still occupied by the peasantry, were still not dependent for their construction upon the services of the skilled mason-architect employed by the aristocracy of Church and Court.

The builders employed by the yeoman were, in fact, the village carpenters or 'wrights' using as their material forest oak.

This was the period of the setting out of the English village as we know it today. The hovels of the Middle Ages, cluttering up the waste land near the manor house, gradually became gathered together in some form of grouping around a village green, pond, or water supply; sometimes in even more orderly fashion along the lanes leading towards the great open fields. Only in the case of the proximity of one of the larger manors, especially if there were a parish church provided, would the settlement become a proper township, or 'village' as we describe it today.

Farmers who had large holdings in the open fields would live in the township in houses set beside a green or lane. The owners of sheep runs, also, would live beside the arable farmers in the township. It was as these groups of houses came within the sphere of operations of the rural builders of the fifteenth century that the villages of today began to take shape.

The roof-tree with its straddling 'crucks' was generally the keystone of the construction. With the shingled roof thus secured against collapse the problem of providing proper walls could be tackled. Material was at hand in the rough boards cut from the sides of the log when it was squared-up into a beam. At first they had been just stuck into the ground—the 'bratticing' which failed to protect the English army at Hastings—but eventually they were being fixed into horizontal beams at top

45

and bottom. By this means screens could be made for internal partitions, or even for external walling as may still be seen in the ancient church of Greensted in Essex.

But with the improvement of joinery technique which one finds towards the end of the twelfth century the boards became replaced by squared timbers, called 'studs', tenoned into the horizontal heads and sills to form properly-framed walls which could have their panels filled or 'nogged' with willow-wattle plastered with clay, or with lumps of field stone set in clay or even mortar. It is this type of framed screen which becomes the fundamental structural factor in the 'half-timber' building of the later Middle Ages—and well afterwards into more sophisticated days.

By the thirteenth century the framed wall was being employed not only in halls but also for the external walling of upper chambers, the ground storey being in masonry. But the use of framed walling in the main structure of any building depended upon the ability of the carpenter to construct a properly-stiffened roof, for the framed screen-wall could never offer the same resistance to overturning roof-thrusts as could a solid wall of stone.

The timber hall of the lesser manor house of the Middle Ages —direct ancestor of the house of the Tudor yeoman and through it the farmhouses and cottages of today—was probably built with very low walling to reduce the risk of collapse under wind pressure. It appears from what little remains of these rustic halls—often, by the way, protected by water-filled moats—that they were normally of four bays in length with the 'dais' occupying one end bay and the usual storerooms the other. From contemporary stone buildings we may deduce that the central feature of the structure would have been a wide timber 'cruck' sweeping across the hall, in place of the more normal pair of posts joined by a horizontal beam which in this position might have been damaged by heat from the fire hearth below it.

Some of the earliest forms of walling were those constructed as screens of wattle daubed with mud or 'cob'—the latter being mud stiffened with some binding or strengthening substance. In its simplest form cob is just road scrapings, in which pieces of straw from animal droppings provide the binding material; it can, of course, be made artificially by mixing chopped straw into mud. Clay, loam, and sand can be mixed by skilled 'cobbers' in the correct proportion; plain chalk will make a good wall.

Mud or cob in its various forms was extensively employed during the Middle Ages for many purposes where there were no facilities for obtaining lime. It was used as plaster, on wall surfaces or on wattle. The method of casting it between boards as if it were the concrete of today was also understood. One simple method of building was to pile the material into long heaps, allow it to 'set', and cut the two faces of the wall straight with a rick-knife.

This 'poor man's masonry' has been in use in England since the Norman Conquest. Even parish churches were constructed of it. Its weakness is that it will dissolve if subjected to continuous damp. Thus it requires 'a good hat and a good pair of shoes'—that is to say a wide thatch with overhanging eaves to keep storm water from streaming down it, and a foundation of rubble stone to protect it from rising damp.

The openings in all these humble structures were necessarily simple in construction. A doorway was simply a gap where the structure, or the filling of a panel in the wall-frame, had been omitted. In a cob wall it was necessary to find some substantial material such as stone or timber balks to line the opening; the lintel would, of course, be a timber beam.

Windows in wooden walls were simply holes or 'wind-eyes' cut in the boarding. In cob—and sometimes in rubble stone walling—a basket was made with a wooden bottom having a large hole cut in this; the basket was then built into the wall as it rose, the boarded 'wind-eye' on the outside of the wall, the basket forming the 'reveal'.

In a framed wall built of 'studs', a window could be framed between the studs and barred with close-set oak bars about two inches square set diagonally. There was of course no glass. In the hovel of the peasant, every item had to be made of humble materials, of which sawn timber would have been the most valuable. Even the owner of a small manor house might have no local builder to assist him in constructing essential features. Thus his hall chimney might have been a bottomless wine-cask fixed to the rafters and with the thatch or shingles trimmed as tightly as possible about it to keep out the rain.

Now that we have some idea of the type of construction at the disposal of the English yeoman of the days when the fourteenth century was turning towards the fifteenth, let us consider the sort of home he wanted.

It would have been a strangely unenterprising sort of fellow who, having brought himself so far up the social scale, would not have based his home to some extent upon that of his one-time lord. With his roof-tree, his crucks, and his walls of board, stud, or cob, he would have no difficulty in providing himself with a miniature hall; the trouble was going to be encountered when he set about constructing the two-storied house which should contain his 'chamber of estate'—the bed-chamber raised above the ground. For him a wall was almost an innovation; one which would rise through two storeys as impossible of realization as a skyscraper. Yet with faith and more than a modicum of good luck the carpenters were soon able to erect buildings of three or four storeys in height, of which each storey was quite independent of its neighbours and itself so completely unstable that it was only held together by the oaken pegs which secured the tenons of its stout timbering. And such buildings weathered the English climate for four centuries and—looking crazier than ever—still survive in their hundreds to this day.

The timbers used as floor joists in the early mediaeval stone buildings had been enormous, a foot or more square in section. The floorboards were generally three inches or so thick. The village wrights of the Tudor period used large balks about a foot square for their main posts and for their floor joists and studs timbers about one-sixth of this section, probably obtained by sawing a log into half and each half into three. Thus these lesser timbers are about six inches by four—usually rather less owing to losses by sawing and smoothing with the adze.

In order to lessen the oppressive appearance of the heavy oaken timbering which ceiled the mediaeval rooms, the edges of both main beams and lesser joists were often moulded in Gothic style. As time went on and timbering became less massive, the mouldings were reduced to simple chamfering, and often omitted altogether from the floor joists. During the eighteenth century, when rooms had become larger and loftier, the chamfering disappeared entirely from beams.

The ends of beams, where these rested on the walling or joined posts, had to remain square; thus the moulding or chamfer had to be stopped a short distance from either end. In the design of these 'stops' the carvers amused themselves by introducing various tricks and motifs; by the seventeenth century, however, the chamfer was simply swept into the square without any fuss.

The 'studs' were set as today with their width across the wall, giving a wall thickness of rather under six inches. They were set close together, at foot centres or so, for strength and to keep the panels small for filling. There were, of course, sturdy ground-sills, generally set on a stone foundation, and a similar timber acted as a head to the framing and had the tops of the studs notched into it.

The floor joists were laid, without regard to the laws of building science, flat on their sides, and were thus very whippy when anyone moved about on the floor they carried. They were set at about foot centres so that there could be no doubt as to the strength of the floor, but this characteristic whippiness of the floor construction led to the most notable feature of Tudor timber construction—the 'jetty'.

The framing-together of the lowermost storey presented no difficulty. Across the heads of opposing side walls the floor joists were laid. Then came the framing of the next storey to be fixed—and this was where the brows of the carpenters began to wrinkle. For as they walked about on the whippy floor-joists, the framing of the upper storey began to jump about, creaking in its joints with each nervous leap. It was the solution of this problem which made possible the erection of those fantastic skyscrapers of Elizabethan England, and at the same time gave the building style of the period that characteristic feature—the 'jetty'. For the carpenters found that if they set each storey out beyond the wall-face of that below, the weight of the upper timberwork upon the jettied-out floor-joists counteracted the weight of persons moving about within the building.

The principle involved is a simple one. A plank set as a bridge across a rivulet might whip so much as to throw the passenger into the water; if a longer plank be procured and its ends weighted down with heavy stones the bridge will be stabilized and will remain firm to cross.

The jetty was an essential feature of the house built by framing up each storey independently and setting one upon another. The Tudor builders often masked the projecting joist ends with moulded timbers; sometimes there was a wide hollow or 'cove' filled with carved ornament (1).

Once accepted as a fundamental structural factor of building with timbers, the jetty became one of the principal aesthetic features of the architecture of the late-fifteenth and sixteenth centuries. The horizontal lines created by each jetty were emphasized in the place of the mediaeval string-course, heralding the strong cornice lines of Renaissance times.

A charming feature of the sixteenth-century jettied house is the elaborately-moulded oriel window tucked in beneath the jetty and providing an important punctuation device in the design, steadying the long sweeps of horizontality which tend to separate the building too completely into its storeys (1).

A more alarming problem was the safety of the roof now perched so ambitiously high above the ground. This had to be solved before the building rose to a second storey, for once a roof became raised upon a wall, and at the same time deprived of the crucks which held the roof-tree, the old tendency to spread and collapse immediately showed itself.

This problem had, of course, been dealt with centuries before by the master-carpenters who had roofed the great churches of the tenth century. The situation had, however, differed from that experienced by the village builders in that these had used to support their roofs loose rafters—either squared timbers or perhaps just poles—laid as individual members from ground to ridge, whereas the sophisticated carpenter used in his roofs a series of 'couples' of rafters joined at the apex. Roofs of any length could be produced by simply setting couples, a foot or so apart, from one end of the building to another. The story of how these fine church and hall roofs were developed by making one couple in eight or so sturdier than the others and eventually using it as a 'principal' upon which could be supported longitudinal timbers which in their turn helped to carry the intermediate rafters is one which is outside the scope of this book, being concerned more with the greater buildings of the country. What is important, however, is to appreciate that even the roofs of the 'King John's houses' had been formed by a series of 'couples' each comprising a pair of rafters securely joined by a collar.

Rafters do not spring direct from a wall-top but rest on a beam called a 'plate' which is laid on the wall and fixed to it in some way so that the spread of the roof shall not force the plate outwards over the edge. In the huge roofs of the cathedrals this thrust was so destructive that it was necessary to tie the plates together across the building by throwing enormous beams called 'tie-beams' across the span.

The same thrust when applied to the side walls of a timber-framed building would very quickly have burst the structure asunder had not the same device of the tie-beam been introduced. And yet another feature was invented in order to stiffen the roof, from which most of the strain upon these crazy buildings derived: a long timber was passed from end to end of the roof immediately beneath the collars and carried upon each tie-beam by a short post called a 'king-post'. It is these little posts, often carved to imitate stone pillars, and generally sprouting curved bracing timbers helping to stiffen the roof, which form such delightful ornaments to the house-roofs of the fifteenth century.

These king-posts appear before the end of the fourteenth century and continue in use until the middle of the sixteenth. An attractive feature of Tudor roofs is the system of timber arches which was provided to serve as 'wind braces'. They only appear after the roof has been divided into bays separated by some form of 'roof truss' and carrying longitudinal purlins and a ridge. This fifteenth century development, used to good effect in church roofs, did not appear in houses until the next century. During the reign of Henry VIII in particular, the high-pitched roofs of the rural halls often had two or more purlins on each side, carried on 'principal rafters' at bay interval and sometimes intermediately as well. Between each horizontal line of timberwork is a row of curved wind braces; charming in decorative effect, their structural purpose is to prevent the whole roof collapsing from wind pressure on a gable end.

The principle of Tudor timber construction was to build each storey separately, with the intervening floor carried out over the lower storey as a 'jetty'; the simplest plan being to lay the floor joists across the narrow way of the building with the jetties running down its long sides. It was also possible to run a large beam—a 'girder' or 'summer'—to join two opposite posts next to the end of the building and lay the joists from this to the end wall so as to have a jetty there as well. From this was developed the 'dragon' (diagonal) beam which bisected the angle of the building and enabled the jetties to be 'mitred' round this. (Fig. 6b). The end of the big dragon beam was supported by a heavy post called a 'teazle post' which was made from a tree trunk set upside down; the thick end was carved into a decorative form merging with the end of the dragon beam (1).

The above description of the constructional methods employed by the builders of the fifteenth century indicates that by this time the 'King John's houses', which during the last two centuries had been the residences of the nobility, were now being copied in timber framing by the English yeomen. At the upper end of the hall, instead of the tall stone gable-end with its two-light window, there now rose the two-storied timber-framed house-end with the chamber floor overhung on a 'jetty'.

The hall itself had long ago profited from roofing developments to an extent that it could now boast walls, either of field-stone, cob, or timber framing; it was in fact the combination of this archaic apartment with a two-storied house attached to its upper end which provided the rich yeoman of the latter part of the fifteenth century with his home. Built for the most part with the profits of the wool trade and the results of mercantile dealings with Flanders and the vast markets of central Europe, many of these early houses, timbered miniatures of the mediaeval manor houses, may be found in the south-eastern counties.

While the fundamental factors which made up the mediaeval manor house were the hall, the chamber on an upper floor, and to a lesser degree the pantry and buttery for the storage of food and drink, the arrangements for the positioning of these did not follow a standard plan. There are, however, three principal variations of the manor house plan. The first is perhaps the nearest to standard in that it followed that of the larger houses: this is the chamber over the parlour at the upper end of the hall and the storerooms in their usual place at the opposite end. What might be called the ecclesiastical plan—for

5. A single-parlour farmhouse of late seventeenth-century date at Eling in Hampshire illustrating the fashion in which the thatch is swept round the gable end in order to avoid long exposed verges of straw and at the same time to provide wall space for an attic window if desired. This is the origin of the 'Sussex hip' (*see* Plate 13).

6. This very humble single-parlour farmhouse of late seventeenth-century date near Somersby in Lincolnshire has no chamber floor so that what would, in a two-storeyed house, have been the parlour was probably here used as a bedchamber.

no other reason than its being found frequently in priests' houses (Fig. 4) and bishops' palaces—is the chamber over the storerooms at the lower end of the hall and no upper-end building at all. The third and most advanced type of manor house has the 'standard' plan with a second chamber over the storerooms (Fig. 6a). All three of these types may be found among the small timber manor houses of the fifteenth and sixteenth centuries.

Wall fireplaces would have been possible in the hall and the parlour ('Full sooty was her bower and eke her hall') but not in the chamber above unless the stack was carried up from the ground. In humbler houses, the side of the chamber next the hall was probably sometimes left open to the warmth of the hall fire below.

The archaism of these houses would undoubtedly have been apparent even to the yeomen of the fifteenth century. Feudalism was for all practical purposes extinct, broken into final ruin with the Wars of the Roses, in the course of which the nobility had led their savage little armies against each other like so many cats of Kilkenny. The feudal magnate, with his vast echoing hall, was becoming unworthy of the honour of imitation. What was now wanted was a more comfortable, more workable home.

The mediaeval hall could never have been a really comfortable room to live in. The nuisance of the fire burning on the central hearth and smoking the place out unless the entrance door was left open had been abated to some extent during the fifteenth century when the wall-fireplace which had always been employed in upper chambers was introduced, on a larger scale, in the hall. Thus there was no longer any real need for the hall to be open to the roof in order to allow the smoke to escape through the vent there provided. It was even possible for a comparatively humble individual who could find someone to build him a stone chimney to construct a house having the hall on the ground floor and the chamber over it—the dignity of a private parlour not for him—and thus provide himself with a compact dwelling of a dignity never before attainable by a man of his standing.

Such are the Tudor country houses which cover the south-eastern counties of England. Within their four framed walls they could be planned internally as taste and means suggested. The hall—which has in effect become the farmhouse kitchen—may have partitioned off it a buttery or dairy; perhaps even a small parlour may be there. Above are probably two chambers

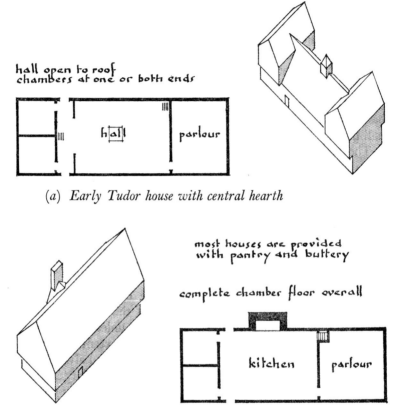

hall open to roof
chambers at one or both ends

hall   parlour

(a) *Early Tudor house with central hearth*

most houses are provided
with pantry and buttery

complete chamber floor overall

kitchen   parlour

(b) *Later Tudor house with fireplace and chimney*

Fig. 6. Yeomen's houses of the Tudor era

one of which was the yeoman's 'chamber of estate' (compare the nautical 'state room' or sleeping cabin) the other being for children and maidservants. There was a sturdy chimney stack attached to one side of the house and having at its base the wide kitchen fireplace.

Yet even well into the sixteenth century it was not always possible to find material and workmanship for the construction of a chimney. Then we find a most delightful type of house having two separate chambers jettied out above each end, one over a parlour and the other above storerooms. Between the two, occupying the middle third of the house, is a tiny hall, very lofty up to the roof which covers the whole structure from end to end. These attractive houses still stand thick in the south-eastern counties, though long ago, of course, the fire which once smouldered on the open hearth was covered over by a Jacobean chimney-stack.

A well-designed house might have the whole group of rooms gathered under one roof. But the memory of the hall with its house at the end—or, perhaps, a two-storied structure at *each* end—remained; thus more often than not the two (or three) units are separately framed and the end units have their own roofs running at right-angles to that of the hall. This gives the charming effect of gables on the main front, instead of at the end, of the house. The dignity of the great chamber was often enhanced by a fine window on the main front, framed by its gable.

These yeomen's houses of the fifteenth and sixteenth centuries, the direct outcome of the wool trade between England and the Continent, are thus limited in their distribution to those regions—East Anglia, the Home Counties, Sussex and Hampshire—which form the hinterland of the commercial littoral—the old 'Saxon Shore' of Roman England.

In all these houses we begin to discover a type of structure planned as an entity, to be contained within four walls instead of as an assemblage of two very ill-assorted neighbours— the large single-storied hall and the tall two-storied house. Thus something of a standardized plan has been evolved for the yeoman's house. Moreover the construction itself is so simple that it too may be said to have been standardized. The walls of timber-framed screens set between head and sill and nogged with some easily-procured filling material are mounted upon rough rubble stone foundations in the ground storey, and balanced upon the jettied-out floor-joists for the upper floor; tied with tie-beams at the top they may easily carry the simple roof-framing (2).

The advantage these houses possessed over all earlier builder-constructed homes was their comparative cheapness, particularly in those regions where oak timber was readily procurable. The story was not quite the same in the stone belt, away from the clay-lands where the forests flourished, for transport in those days was almost too difficult for contemplation. (It was for this very reason that one did not find good stone houses away from quarry areas except where some affluent personage or community had been able to meet the enormous expense of bringing the stone to the site.) But building technique had changed; there was no need nowadays to go to the trouble of spending a year or two in gathering flints or field-stone and then waiting patiently for the arrival of some journeyman mason who could help with the corners and the openings; one's village carpenter could fell a few oaks and run up a respectable house. Thus the stoneless regions of the south-east began to outbuild the once-favoured areas and with their timber framing to found a new and vigorous style in English architecture which was to spread throughout the country in the same fashion as that inaugurated by the mediaeval masoncraft of Somerset, Northamptonshire, or Yorkshire.

It will be noted that the 'half-timber' house was essentially the product of a builder, a practical job owing nothing to forms of embellishment such as had been developed by the masons. Thus when it came to the ornamentation of an opening—the lintel of a doorway, the head of a window—the carpenters had perforce to copy from their rival colleagues. But by the middle of the sixteenth century they had abandoned this copyism, content to let their carpentry speak for itself.

The frames of timber houses were made at the saw-pit, the timbers fitted together, the joints coded with incised symbols, and the frames knocked to pieces again for transport to the building site. The code used was a numerical one. Arabic numerals did not appear in England until the Elizabethan Renaissance (for this reason it was quite impossible for the mediaeval engineer or accountant to perform the simplest sum without using a chequer board and counters) so the carpenters used Roman numerals, cutting them into the wood with strokes of a chisel. These coded joints may be seen in all old timber buildings but some of the numerals they represent may be difficult to understand as the illiteracy of the inscribers caused them to use various combinations of I, V and X without regard to strict Latinity.

Once arrived at the building site, it was up to the house-owner to get the frame erected. Neighbours usually helped with this, hauling the timbers and made-up frames to their appropriate positions. A communal effort like this doubtless called for celebration when the job was completed; until quite recently it was the custom when building a house for the builder's foreman to fix a small Union Jack to the ridge timber as soon as this was placed in position and call attention to it at the next visit of the prospective owner, who somehow always seemed to understand what was expected of him.

There was probably some sort of control of building. Yet it seems also to have been the custom that if a house-builder could get his frame erected and the ridge timber fixed between dusk and dawn, the structure was accepted as a *fait accompli*.

The right of a man to build and occupy a house on a particular site might depend on his standing with his neighbours. Not only might they refuse to help him with its erection but they might later on ask him to go away and take his house with him. If he delayed they might knock out the pins themselves, tie ropes to the timbers, and pull the whole structure down. It is interesting to note that even today when we demolish a house with a pneumatic drill we still talk of *pulling* it down.

Let us for a moment consider the distribution of houses in the English countryside of those days, in order that we may gain some insight into the probable antiquity of those small houses and 'cottages' remaining at the present time.

During the earlier mediaeval period, the only houses worth the name would have been the residences of the lords of manors, varying in excellence of construction from the important—perhaps fortified—manor house down to the humble home of the owner of some poorly endowed manor. The hovels of small-holders and peasants would have been erected on waste land nearby, or along the lanes leading away to the great common fields of the manor. These groups of houses would constitute the 'township' of mediaeval days. The township attached to a rich manor might attract the attention of itinerant vendors of such necessities as cloth or household goods; such a township

57

might then become a market town though still, in our modern eyes, a village, and in civic status far below that of a city with its streets of shops, merchants' houses, and perhaps even buildings for administrative purposes unknown to the rural township.

Small isolated manor houses were the first 'farmhouses', as we know them today settled in the corners of the English countryside. The yeomen farmers of Tudor days built their homes in the township; those village 'cottages' we see nowadays are for the most part the homes of late-mediaeval or Tudor farmers whose actual holdings were scattered in strips throughout the great common fields of their day.

Not until the rearrangement of the common fields into compact individual holdings, which took place largely during the eighteenth century, did the farmers begin to build farmhouses on their farm lands. Thus the isolated farmhouses of today are usually either of Georgian origin (though possibly in seventeenth-century building style) or else represent small manor houses dating originally from quite early mediaeval days.

While the timber-framed building style flourished for the most part in the south-eastern counties it spread in notable fashion through the cities of England. Most of these commercial centres were by this time strangling in the grip of massive fortifications laid out to protect a far smaller population than they now encompassed. The solution to inevitable overcrowding was the usual one—to build upwards. The new form of construction enabled this to be done, especially as the craziness of its mechanics could in some measure be overcome through the support each town house gave to those adjoining it. But each storey had to be jettied-out over that below, so that houses facing each other across the narrow alleys of Anglo-Saxon cities were apt almost to support each other across the way!

These towering merchants' houses of the early part of the sixteenth century form the counterpart of the country houses of the yeomen and contribute most notably to the middle-class architecture of their era. The key to their form is the result of restrictions placed upon mediaeval urban building, partly through the retention of original building plots generally less than twenty feet in frontage, and also the fact that the town could not expand beyond the perimeter of its protecting wall of enceinte.

The street frontage of each house was usually occupied by a shop, that is to say an apartment in which the goods of the merchant were seen and bought by visiting customers. There was little room for any form of display, the shop window being merely one rather larger than normally required to give light; beside it was the shop doorway of normal form. The goods were stored at the rear of the ground floor. In the yard at the back of the house were the kitchen, the primitive sanitary arrangements, and probably a stable for the merchant's pony.

Jettied out above the shop would be the owner's hall, above it his chamber and guest room, while garrets in the roof would house his domestic and commercial staff. Such were the timber 'skyscrapers' which contributed to the skyline of the English market towns of the fourteenth and fifteenth centuries.

The intensification of building activity which accompanied the development of timber technique, and the consequent expansion of the country's building potential, began to extend the scope of the industry's activities into the realm of public buildings. The public building was simply the private house with its apartments made available for the use of the public. Thus the hall of the house might become the public room of an inn, or perhaps a town hall or a schoolroom. There was no existing model for any specialized building to follow.

The inn had its common hall, with perhaps a parlour for more important visitors, while on the floor above were bedchambers. Accommodation had, of course, to include stabling for animals, situated at the rear of the main building and reached through an entry from the street frontage. It was this entry which thenceforth became the principal feature of the inn-front, becoming enlarged during the seventeenth century in order to accommodate travelling coaches. At this period the usual form of the town inn was the double plot with twin gables rising above and the entry contrived in the framing of the ground storey, on the site of the party wall and flanked by hall and parlour. The kitchen, as in the private house, might be in an annexe to the rear of the hall.

Some town houses had their own back yards for stabling,

kitchen, and privvy; even the ordinary single-plot house could often contrive a narrow passage leading thence to the street. In this design we can detect the germ of the terrace house of the late-seventeenth century.

As we explore the streets of our mediaeval towns today and enter their houses, inns, and shops, we cannot fail to notice how many late-mediaeval buildings are still standing behind later façades. We may see great posts, frames, and beams still playing their part in carrying massive solars and high-pitched roofs thick with oak. For perhaps five centuries these timbers have carried their loads undismayed.

Behind a modern showcase, a door flanked by a juke-box opens on to a steep timber caracole at the head of which one enters a series of apartments separated by boarded bratticing and ceiled by close-set floor-joists six inches wide. Perhaps there is a tangled foliage of oaken trusses, purlins, king-posts, wavy wind-braces, and all the panoply of a mediaeval roof.

By the accession of Henry VIII the timber-building technique of England had reached its zenith. The day of the mason had passed into twilight; even in the stone-producing regions the craft was mainly employed in the maintenance of castles and great houses. The once-powerful monastic houses were falling into a state of neglect and could provide a livelihood for few masons; their art was declining into a condition from which Gothic comeliness was steadily passing away.

The event in English history which produced the greatest effect on the architectural development of the country was certainly the dissolution of the monastic houses. And this is apart from the economic revolution which it caused by redistributing the vast estates of the mediaeval church among hitherto landless folk.

It is true that the Church no longer shared with the Crown and the nobility the monopoly of building potential in the land. But many of the richer monasteries were still engaged in building projects; moreover the huge establishments were in constant need of repair and had maintenance squads employed for the purpose. At a blow all this ceased. A large block of building potential was released for employment by others—in particular by the new grantees of monastic lands who were wanting homes in which to maintain their new-won state.

7. The massive central chimney-stack of this seventeenth century farmhouse at Grantchester in Cambridgeshire has survived the conversion of the building into cottages and a shop.

8. This one-time farmhouse at Great Bardfield in Essex has been deprived of its lower parlour during the eighteenth century to make a carriage way through to the back of the house. The whole of the upper end of the house beyond the great chimney-stack was removed and replaced by a complete Georgian house with a new main entrance. The older portion is now divided off into cottages. Note the little touch of Regency Gothic over the windows; the bays are mid-nineteenth century.

The vast monastic settlements themselves became almost inexhaustible quarries for building materials. Hundreds of tons of lead were quickly stripped from the roofs of enormous churches, spacious refectory halls, and the long two-storied houses of the vanished monks. There was lead for a thousand homes which had been hitherto roofed in tile or even thatch. There were whole sections of timber roofs to be taken down and re-used, or at least resold timber by timber for the manufacture of house frames. There were floor joists and beams and thick mediaeval boarding and framed partitions for sale by the house-breakers. In the end the huge structures were undermined and tumbled into heaps of rubble for use by persons needing stone homes or for adding chimney-stacks to existing wooden ones. There was rubble for filling holes in town streets and for building retaining walls in place of eroded earthen slopes.

For the first time in English history, ordinary folk were able to wander at will through vast buildings the like of which they had never before seen. While the lead was being stripped from the great churches they could stare in amazement at the soaring roofs of the monastic refectories, wander through the long dormitories where the monks had slept in a comfort undreamed of by the dweller in hovels of wattle and daub. Now he was free of the dining-hall of my lord abbot, his parlour with its ceiling of carved beams, his bedchamber with the tester protecting his bed from down-draughts. The yokel could see for the first time capacious fireplaces, lavatories for the washing of hands, sanitary conveniences with water-borne sewage such as the monks had been using for centuries. While the majority of our peasant sightseers would have been mainly concerned with what they could loot, more than a few must have considered what they could emulate. And for those who had the means, the creator of all this magnificence, the English building trade, was now released for re-employment by lay hands.

The mediaeval hall may have been a cheerful spot in winter, with its huge bonfire always burning on the central hearth. But it may not have always been so with parlour or chamber, for these apartments needed fireplaces of stone, with chimney flues to carry off the smoke, if they were to be even partially heated. Such features could only be built by masons, those rare and expensive tradesmen not always detachable from their lordly patrons in castle and abbey. But the dissolution of the monasteries freed large numbers of masons, which may have been the reason for the later Tudor era becoming the Age of Chimneys. The great mansions of the day were expanding in all directions with wings of 'lodgings' for the accommodation of guests and their retinues. It was an age when a display of hospitality was required of all who wished to be considered of importance; the King himself, and the great Queen who followed him, were tireless in availing themselves of this ubiquitous hospitality.

The parlour and chamber of the day had to have a fireplace for heating. This was true not only of the great mansions but the country homes also. The chimney stack with its chimney arch or beam, and its flue ending in an attractive-looking cap, became the popular feature of the period, being added everywhere outside the existing walls of buildings. The central hearths of halls became obsolete and were replaced by cavernous fireplaces, often with magnificently ornamented surrounds, set in one of the external walls. Two-storied stacks, containing fireplaces for parlour and chamber, were added everywhere where they were not already existing—for the wall-fireplace, originating in the eleventh century, had always been an essential feature of the great chamber of the mediaeval mansion and had been added to the chambers of lesser homes wherever possible.

The mediaeval fireplace was contained in an excrescence built out from the side wall of the structure where the walling was not so high as at the gable end. In the absence of lead for a chimney gutter, a small lateral roof was formed to join the stack to the main roof which was swept across to cover it. In well-built stone houses the chimney stack might be incorporated in a gable end; the feature appears in the Cotswold building of the seventeenth century. But for general purposes, the gable stack belongs to the buildings of the eighteenth and nineteenth centuries with their efficiently-constructed walling of brick or stone.

The literature of the Tudor Age is full of comments on the universal appeal of the fireplace and its exterior manifestation, the chimney, which must have had at that time much of the social significance indicated by the sprouting television aerial which gives it today the ultimate distinction.

The mediaeval chamber fireplace had been a comparatively shallow recess with the hearth projecting into the room and the smoke gathered into a heavy stone canopy carried on massive brackets or 'corbels'. These 'chimneys' disappeared during the fifteenth century and the more deeply-recessed fireplace with its flue contained in an external chimney stack became the universal form of this feature.

Tudor fireplaces were usually framed in stone by skilled masons and often ornamented by carvers. The fireplace opening was sometimes arched over but more often a massive stone lintel was provided, cut into the shape of a very flat four-centred arch. The 'spandrels' at the two corners were usually filled with some carved symbol such as a coat of arms or a merchant's mark.

The Tudor window was of mediaeval type with mullions, either made of freestone or with the masonry technique copied in timber. The head of each light was shaped to form an arch, at first four-centred with a slight point, by Henry VIII's reign three-centred with none. The glazing was in the small diamond-shaped panes called 'quarries' held in position by the lead strips known as 'calms' (pronounced 'cames'). Opening lights were hand-wrought iron casements hung on hooks and secured by ornamental 'cockspur' fasteners; the leadwork was wired to holes in the iron frames as it was to the ironwork of the large stone-mullioned window.

The Tudor door was of mediaeval type with heavy vertical planking on the outside and a series of sturdy horizontal 'ledgers' inside to keep the whole construction together. The door was hung on hooks driven into the frame and secured by draw-bars of wood or iron. Heavy locks were also in use.

We have now seen how the building boom of the late fifteenth century, continuing into the reign of Henry VIII, received a tremendous fillip from the dissolution of the monastic houses and the consequent release of large quantities of materials as well as skilled craftsmen. A still more important result of the Dissolution was the creation of a new class of professional men —the Surveyors who took upon themselves the task of surveying the vast estates before their reallocation. Such monastic buildings as were saved from the general holocaust were also measured up by these surveyors. From their measurements they had to set out the plan of the building and often design and set out the form of its conversion to secular use. While measuring their buildings they could hardly avoid discovering a good many things about building construction; thus with this knowledge combined with experience in planning they were well on the way to becoming architects themselves. And they were, in fact, the first architects of the English Renaissance.

CHAPTER III

Elizabethan and Jacobean Standardized Planning

❈

The Elizabethan Age was the English echo of the Italian Renaissance, the movement which accompanied the Reformation and began to divert cultural achievement away from ecclesiastical and towards secular patronage. The movement was thus social as well as cultural, architecture being treated not only as an aesthetic exercise but as popular science. A hundred years before Elizabeth's accession, the Roman architect Alberti had published a book on matters connected with building; the craft of the builder thus became acknowledged as a subject for scholarship.

One of the highlights of the Tudor era had been the meeting between Henry VIII of England and Francis I of France at the Field of the Cloth of Gold. The Court Architect of France at the time was none other than Vignola, author of a work on the Orders of Architecture and one of the principal disseminators of the Renaissance style in western Europe.

By the reign of Elizabeth, mediaeval symbolism had been replaced in England by the new spirit of the Renaissance. Not that the architectural details of the new style had penetrated into the country in any but weirdly misconceived form, but the importance of architectural design had been realized and the buildings of the future were henceforth to be properly planned as considered entities before even the foundations were laid.

The architect with his drawing-board had to be brought into the picture. The nucleus of the profession already existed in the mid-sixteenth century surveyors who had measured up and drawn the plans of the derelict monastic houses and their estates before these were divided up amongst secular grantees. (One of the most notable of these surveyors was John Thorpe, many of whose drawings have fortunately been preserved.)

Having no graduated scales with which to work, the surveyors drew up their plans on paper which they had ruled into squares. They knew the elements which went to make up the plan of a mansion house, and how large each of these should be. They were familiar with the elevational details of the various features—doors, windows, and chimneys—which gave the house its external appearance; what they had to do was to devise a tidy arrangement of these items and provide a plan which would suit this. Not a simple exercise for an untrained man. . . . Especially when one of the primary rules of Renaissance design was that the housefront must be symmetrical about its central entrance feature—no matter how asymmetrical the most convenient plan might have turned out. It was on such problems that the Elizabethan surveyors cut their teeth, losing little time before producing the lovely mansion houses of their glorious era. Shakespeare has described how the architects of the day drew the 'plot' or plan, and thence prepared the 'model' or elevational aspect of the building. So by his day it is clear that the architectural profession had been firmly founded and knew how to plan and construct as large a building as might be required, in an orderly Renaissance manner.

The form of the Elizabethan mansion with its two wings and central porch—the whole forming an 'E' on plan though this is not, as is sometimes supposed, a cunning device of the architects to flatter the Queen—is too well known to require discussion in these pages. What we are concerned with is the form of the middle-class yeoman's house of the same period.

By the middle of the sixteenth century, the mediaeval arrangement of hall and parlour with chamber above had settled down into a simple rectangular plan, two storeys in height with a parlour floor below and a chamber floor above. The universal use of the wall fireplace had enabled the hall to be ceiled over and the chamber floor continued across it. (Fig. 6b). Jettied all round and with finely carved 'teazle posts' at each corner, the Late Tudor farmhouse was a well-designed building with nothing left of the muddle of mediaeval conglomeration.

The hall still remained, but it was a simple ground-floor room which had in fact become the farmhouse kitchen-living-room.

A problem with these fully-jettied houses was how to manage the ascent to the upper floor. With the old open hall, a steep ladder-like stair—almost vertical—rose out of the end of this to the chamber door. But a stair could not be made to pass through the floor itself, as the modern method of 'trimming' floor-joists to make an opening was unknown and indeed would have been very difficult to employ in a springy jettied floor. Some kind of small enclosure—a sort of cupboard—had therefore to be constructed, to enclose the stair and at the same time to support the severed ends of the two or three floor-joists disturbed by its passage.

These houses still displayed the massive form of construction which employed closely-packed timbers enclosing very narrow panels nogged with wattle-and-daub. But at the beginning of the last quarter of the century, when the threat of Spanish invasion was becoming a source of anxiety, the Queen's government began to wonder whether the denudation of the country's forests was going to leave enough over for the shipyards. This was the period of emergence of the surveyor-architects, and doubtless they were consulted over the matter. Before the Armada actually appeared the order had gone forth for timber rationing and the devising of a less extravagant form of construction.

Thus it was during the last quarter of the sixteenth century that the closely-studded frames of mediaeval days began to be abandoned; more scientifically designed frames with horizontal timbers at window-sill level, fewer vertical studs, and square panels were substituted. Such frames would not have been strong enough without diagonal bracing; these were wrought from waste timber, pieces left over, or pieces out of straight. Towards the end of the century, the house-wrights began to discover a new use for curved braces, arranging these into charming patterns framing the plastered panels and turning the whole house-front into a fret of tracery.

It was at this period that the new class of yeomen began to expand away from the south and east of the country into the Midlands. Leaping the timberless Cotswolds, where the stone-building technique of mediaeval times still survived, the carpenters soon obtained a hold on the north-west Midlands where the Renaissance had not yet penetrated. As the sixteenth century turned into the seventeenth, the mature Elizabethan timber style of the south-eastern counties spread through Worcestershire and Herefordshire towards the Marches of Wales. With the spirit of the Middle Ages still inspiring them, the carpenters of Cheshire, Shropshire, Lancashire and neighbouring shires were soon covering their houses with an exquisite diaper of swept and foliated braces, creating that lovely style of whitewashed panels framed in old black timbering which we know as 'magpie'.

During the Elizabethan era a new apartment appears, augmenting the simple living accommodation provided for the use of himself and his family by the owner of a Tudor great house. The disadvantage of being the Lord of the Manor and sitting in—often draughty—splendour at your high table was that the kitchen was at the other end of the house and your food arrived cold. The solution was to abandon that impressive feudal custom of dining in hall and to provide yourself with a private room—the winter parlour, the origin of our dining-room of today.

The provision of a family dining-room—an amenity long overdue—had first been attempted, towards the end of the fifteenth century, by throwing out a room beside the upper end of the hall and entered from the end of the dais. (Fig. 5). While this gave the required privacy, however, it made the journey from kitchen to table of even longer duration, so that the family's soup arrived colder than ever. Thus it was at the lower end of the hall—an innovation, indeed, by mediaeval standards —that the Elizabethans eventually sited their winter parlour. In doing so they gave great delight to their architects, striving to achieve that balance of structures, at either end of the principal feature, their Renaissance souls so deeply desired.

All these parlours, with their chambers over, had to have a sufficiency of wall fireplaces to heat them. These fireplaces, and the chimney-stacks containing them, had to be built of stone, or where this and masons to work it were unprocurable, in brick.

Bricks had long been used in East Anglia, brought over as ballast in trading ships from the Low Countries where brick was the normal building material. During the sixteenth

9. A parlour-less farmhouse of seventeenth-century date at Salford Priors in Warwickshire having a single gable-stack to house the fireplace of the living room and two bedchambers over this.

10. This fine late seventeenth-century double-parlour house at Charmouth in Dorset has had its front 'Georgianized' during the eighteenth century. Note the position of the entrance doorway at the lower end of the living room. During the nineteenth century the two parlours with their chambers over were provided with tall bay windows of urban type.

century the surveyors had been searching for deposits of brick earth, and by the end of the century the stoneless regions of the country were becoming well served by brickyards. Fine houses were being built of this humble material; the chimney-stacks of the yeomen's farmhouses were for the most part brick-built.

When James I succeeded to the throne of England he was shocked at the appearance of his new capital. Coming from stone-built Edinburgh he was amazed to find the narrow streets of London lined with crazy skyscrapers jettied out again and again to nudge each other across the way. Appalled at the fire-risk, he had an order promulgated that in future the city house-fronts were to be built of brick. Announcing himself as a new Augustus, he said he would change the face of London 'from stykkes to brykkes'.

From this time the jetty was doomed. Its disadvantages were obvious. The builders therefore began to abandon the form of construction which built each storey separately and balanced one upon the other. Henceforth they erected what constructional engineers today call 'balloon frames', in which the main posts rise right up through more than one storey and support the feet of the rafters direct from the ground (12). The new panelled and braced form of timber construction enabled such walls to be framed without difficulty.

The problem was how to check the whippiness of the floor timbers—still being laid, in mediaeval fashion, flat on their sides—after the counter-balancing weight of the upper storey had been removed.

The difficulty had appeared as soon as the wide-span halls of the Elizabethans had been covered over with an upper storey. In mediaeval times it had been encountered in all wood floors carried across a stone building, but then it had simply been met by using very heavy timbers. With any wide-span building, something was needed to support its floor-joists in mid span: this was done by running heavy cross beams across the building and making these carry the floor beams themselves at right-angles, these secondary beams holding up the middles of the joists. Before timber economy became necessary, such arrangements of floor timbers could be used to make charming ceiling patterns; each member being moulded along its edges, 'stopped' at ends and junctions, and carved at intersections with heraldic and other devices. (It is said that an intersection at the upper end of a parlour ceiling might be marked with a Tudor Rose, to which a speaker might point when emphasizing that some observation was to be considered as being *sub rosa*.)

The principal posts of a jettyless timber house of the Jacobean era were joined in opposing pairs by heavy beams—'summers' or 'girders'—set at first-floor level. Between the centres of these beams was fixed a series of others passing down the long axis of the building and halving the span of the floor joists. Unfortunately the main beams were seldom strong enough and, having the secondary beams mortised into them, were apt to crack across the middle. Today most of these shaky intersections are held together by crude hand-wrought iron straps.

The heavy beam passing down the axis of a building instead of spanning it was an innovation which had wide-sweeping results. The alarming effects produced by mortising it into the transverse beams indicated that some other means of carrying it would have to be devised.

In mediaeval times, only walls carrying roof-timbers—in other words external walls—were constructed of load-bearing materials. Internal partitioning was provided by making wooden screens of vertical boards housed at top and bottom into horizontal heads and sills. Each board was set at a distance from its neighbour and the gap covered by another board. This is the 'brattice' or board-wall used since Anglo-Saxon days and the source of all subsequent screen, door, and panelling construction; it was used as a stockade round the ramparts of a Norman timber castle and may be seen today in rustic outbuildings.

In old houses, widths of boarding, whether in floor or brattice, give an indication of early date. The late-mediaeval board was often eighteen inches in width and even in Georgian days boards often hold to a foot or more wide. The coverboards in bratticing are much narrower and often lightly moulded.

Where an internal load-bearing partition was required, whether the main building was of stone, brick, or a timber frame, the partition would often be of timber-framed construction. Thus with the introduction into ordinary housebuilding technique of the longitudinal or spinal beam as a floor

70

support, where an internal chimney-stack could not be used as a bearing—as in a two-parlour house—a framed partition had to be inserted across the building to carry it. Thus the internal partitioning of a small house is set out as part of the structural planning and not always for living convenience.

A notable feature of the Elizabethan great house is the multiplicity of its apartments compared with that of the house of late-mediaeval days. While lacking the sprawl of the mediaeval building, the compact product of the surveyor provided a multitude of chambers for the accommodation of guests as well as for household staff. Moreover, once the hall had been ceiled over and the mediaeval open roof finally abandoned, house owners began to explore the potentialities of the roof space as a third storey.

The use of the tie-beam in later mediaeval roofs as a support for the king-post had already suggested the laying of a floor at this level. The trouble was the obstruction caused by the timbering of the roof itself. By the Elizabethan period, the king-post with its spray of curved braces had become modified and now formed part of a 'truss' based upon the tie-beam and having 'principal rafters' which carried longitudinal timbers— purlins and the ridge itself—by which the individual rafters, no longer paired in 'couples', were supported.

In mediaeval times the household servants slept on pallets ranged along the side walls of the hall, like soldiers in a barrack room. This kind of accommodation was not suitable for the house-servant of Elizabethan times; nor indeed was there any hall large enough to sleep them in the ordinary house of the day. The solution to this problem was to utilize the new storey within the roof. Thus was devised the attic or garret, thenceforth to be found in most houses as the old open mediaeval roofs became hidden away for ever from the chamber floors as well as from that of the hall.

In these garrets slept the house-servants, ranged as before down the sides of the roof under the eaves. As the king-posts would have obstructed any central gangway they were abolished and replaced by a new kind of construction having a pair of 'queen posts', joined at their tops by the collar which, with the tie-beam and principal rafters, formed a well-constructed roof-truss spanning the building at bay interval. These trusses

71

invariably carried the longitudinal timbers known as purlins and a central ridge timber. The mediaeval 'couples' entirely disappeared and were replaced by a series of independent rafters spanning from wall-top to ridge and supported intermediately by one or more purlins.

These garrets could have been woefully comfortless places, unheated, and unlit except at gable ends. The most striking feature of contemporary French great houses was the 'dormer' window trimmed through the rafters of the roof. This was beyond the capabilities of the Elizabethan house-builders, but the more efficient construction now employed enabled them to devise small lateral roofs ending in gablets ranged along the side walls of the building and filled with small windows. Other small gablets could be run to a convenient chimney-stack so that even a fireplace could be incorporated in the garret. Many-gabled houses were thus a feature of the Jacobean era and in the hands of the Cotswold masons of the seventeenth century became one of the delights of English domestic architecture.

One of the charming features of the smaller English house is the way in which the rural builders seized upon some architectural feature of the great house and converted it to their own idiom. Thus the gablet of Jacobean days, when utilized by the rustic builder for the purpose of lighting attics, became just an upward swelling of the wall round which the thatch or tiling swept to form 'eyebrows' framing the tiny windows (12). Thus even in the humblest home the attic storey could be decently lit without recourse to too much architectural effort.

The important factor to note is that by the end of the sixteenth century the small house had become three-storied, by including within its accommodation the old open roof of mediaeval days. In one century of the English Renaissance the old open hall had been trebled in its accommodation by inserting between its floor and roof two additional floors. Thus the last vestige of the mediaeval arrangement vanished and the house became in its general form similar to the country house of the present day.

The introduction of the multi-storey house necessitated the provision of good access between the floors. In the larger houses a square tower was added to contain the great stair which passed in straight flights—three to each storey—round its walls.

72

Balusters—a popular innovation from Renaissance Europe—supported a heavy handrail which was itself tenoned into sturdy newel-posts; these also served to carry the raking 'strings' into which the steps themselves were housed. The early newels were tall posts passing right up the stair at each of its internal angles.

The architectural history of the English house follows an unbroken sequence from mediaeval times to the era of the Regency, as from the smaller Elizabethan mansion the 'manorial' type of farmhouse develops into the gracious country house of the eighteenth century and the yeoman's timber-built home becomes the Georgian cottage. But during the seventeenth century, the regular evolutionary process becomes partly obscured owing to the emergence of a special type of house designed to provide conveniently-planned homes for the expanding middle class of yeoman farmers. Beginning at a period when there was an undoubted shortage of housing, these standardized homes sprang up in great numbers and for more than a century constituted by far the major proportion of the houses to be met with in England.

By the beginning of the seventeenth century the English house-builders had already begun to expand their custom by building houses for the farmers of the countryside. These, still pre-fabricated as in Tudor days, were now being standardized in plan as simple rectangular structures having four walls of framework built around the latest architectural invention, an *internal* chimney-stack. (Hitherto chimney-stacks had been projections from an outside wall, but the abandoning of jetties, and the reorganization of the arrangements for carrying floor joists, had at last enabled these to be 'trimmed' round a central stack.)

The standard late-Elizabethan or Jacobean farmhouse is thus a rectangular structure divided into two unequal portions separated by a massive chimney-stack.

The chimney-stack being not only the principal feature of the house but also its most expensive—it had to be built by a mason, 'white' or 'red' (brick)—it was this structure which was first erected. A standard form of stack was agreed upon for universal use. On plan it began as three walls forming an H, the cross-bar representing the axis of the stack which was set across the building and had on either side of it the two fireplaces

73

serving hall and parlour. (Fig. 7). Chimney beams or arches spanned these openings, and the stack continued upwards to open out again into two fireplaces for heating chambers over hall and parlour, after which its flues were carried up to emerge through the roof in a cluster of four chimneys—upon which the designer was encouraged to lavish his skill in order to provide the house with a crowning glory. The Elizabethan or Jacobean chimney cluster is still one of the most notable features of our domestic architecture and represents perhaps the most charming of all vernacular contributions to the Era of the Renaissance.

The Elizabethan fireplace is, of course, the most important ornamental feature of the interior of the great house of the period. Framed up in the curious half-digested Renaissance of the period, this treatment was continued above to form an elaborate carved overmantel, usually including a series of arched recesses or niches. The farmhouse fireplace was of much simpler form, either dressed in stonework as in Tudor days, or with a massive oaken chimney beam which imitated the stone prototype. In the south-east, where brick technique was more developed, the fireplace was sometimes entirely framed in moulded bricks. In its simplest form, the Elizabethan fireplace has jambs of stone or brick and a massive oaken chimney beam which may or may not show some attempt at ornament.

An important feature is the ironwork attached to the fireplace. The iron foundries of Sussex, in particular, turned out quantities of ornamental plates for the protection of the brickwork at the back of the fireplace. These 'firebacks' began to appear in the last quarter of the sixteenth century.

Of earlier date than the fireback is the firedog. This is a device for keeping large logs—the 'cordwood', four feet in length—from rolling out of the fireplace into the room. Having an origin far back in mediaeval times, it continues in use as long as open fireplaces exist and only goes out of use during the late eighteenth century when cast-iron 'interior' grates for coal burning appear.

The stack was of considerable thickness—perhaps eight to ten feet—and thus spaces were left on either side of it, next the long walls of the house. The space on the front elevation of the house became the entrance lobby; into it led the front door and out of it doors to kitchen and parlour. The other space contained the staircase; either a fan-shaped caracole or a complete 'newel-stair' having a central pole into which were housed heavy oaken steps. (Fig. 7).

From the end of the sixteenth century onwards, the 'standardized' farmhouse with its central stack becomes the typical type of rural residence. These are not only found in the

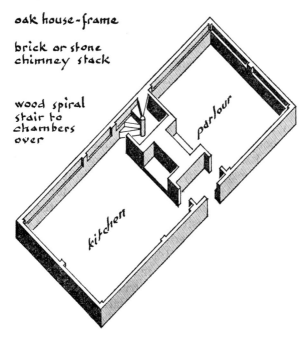

Fig. 7. Elizabethan/Jacobean standard farmhouse-axonometric plan of ground floor

depths of the country but lining the village streets, in the same way as their earlier brethren with the jetties and external wall-stacks. They may vary in size but the fundamental layout is always the same.

Two basic units of measurement are involved. One is the span of the building, probably from sixteen to twenty feet across. Then there is the bay unit, possibly twelve feet but perhaps as much as sixteen. The building is usually about three bays long, of which one is given to the parlour, one and a half to the

75

kitchen-living-room, and the remaining half bay contains the great stack, the entrance lobby, and the spiral stair. There may be eight principal posts, and in wide buildings two more at the gable ends supporting the ends of the median beams carrying the floor joists. Probably there will be two extra posts marking off the half bay containing the chimney, and carrying a cross-beam which forms one of the 'trimmers' carrying the edge of the floor past the great stack and the open stair well.

It will be found, however, that not every house-builder of the seventeenth century could afford a parlour to his house, thus having perforce to content himself with a sadly truncated structure and what should have been a central stack tacked on to the upper end of his kitchen with just the one fireplace in it instead of the back-to-back pair ((9) Fig. 8a). There are many such humble houses—houses to be sure, and *not* cottages—scattered about the villages and the countryside of England.

The framed walls of these houses show an arrangement of square panels separated by comparatively light timbers. There is some bracing in the upper panels next the tops of the main posts, but the whole house-frame has been so strengthened by the existence of the massive central stack that there could have been no fear of anything seriously affecting its rigidity (17).

The best type of mediaeval house was roofed with clay tiles; the yeoman's farmhouse had to make do with a thatch of straw or reed. It is very difficult to construct a gable end in thatch as the wind and rain get under the material and lift it and so begins the deterioration of the roof. The only successful thatch is one which passes all round the building and has eaves all round. The early rectangular houses of the Tudor period were roofed in this fashion with 'hips' at each angle. This was difficult to construct in mediaeval times, when roofs were built in 'couples', but the king-post form of construction enabled diagonal or 'hip' rafters to be laid and short lengths of 'jack rafters' attached to these so as to ease the roof face round the angles of the building.

The steeper the pitch, the more weathertight the roof. But the pitch of the main roof has to be kept within limits to avoid excessive height. With a tiled roof the end pitch must be the same to keep the courses true, but the end pitch of a thatched roof may be twice as steep and often is so.

76

11. Rural architecture of south-western type at Selworthy in Somerset. Built of whitewashed rubble stone, absence of clay tiles for roofing necessitates the use of straw thatch. The external chimney-stack and the mediaeval-type casement windows remain in these regions until well into the eighteenth century.

12. A mid-seventeenth-century three-bay single-parlour farmhouse at Cropthorne in Worcestershire built with concern for timber economy on a wide-panelled 'balloon frame' with its bracing cunningly extended upwards to frame gablets lighting the chamber storey. Note the position of the entrance doorway next the chimney-stack; in this example a main post has been clumsily cut away to accommodate it.

With the coming use of the roof space for accommodation, the hipped end had to be abandoned in order to provide space for windows in the end wall. This resulted in the invention of the 'Sussex hip' an ingenious arrangement whereby the gable wall was allowed to run up to the head of the gable window, and was then 'hipped back' so that the weakest part of the gable—its apex—was well protected and the length of exposed 'verge', where the thatch overhung the gable, reduced to the minimum (5) (13).

The mediaeval type of window was the only one known at this period. The frame of stonework, and the mullions, were simply reproduced with moulded timbers and the lights filled by the familiar leaded glazing; with, however, rectangular panes replacing the old 'quarries'. The Tudor builders still provided arched heads to the lights: first low four-centred arches, and then three-centred with no point. But the Renaissance insistence upon a square head had the effect of abolishing this last trace of mediaevalism and making all lights square-topped.

Some Elizabethan windows were several lights in width. But there was a limit to the length of a mullion, for English oak is a very lively timber and will warp and break glass unless its freedom to do so is restricted. So if the Elizabethans needed a tall window they had to introduce the horizontal 'transom'. Some large windows had two transoms; the important window lighting the dais of the great hall was usually multi-stage.

An interesting type of Tudor window which continued in use for centuries was the shop window. This was protected by a large external shutter, hinged at the bottom, which when opened out formed the 'stall-board', or counter for displaying merchandise. A number of decayed wool towns in East Anglia can still show examples of sixteenth-century shop windows.

The entrance doorway of an Elizabethan mansion was its principal architectural feature. Set in the outer wall of a porch which was carried up for the full height of the building, it was generally round-arched and flanked by somewhat naïve versions of the Classical Orders. The doorway of a timber house of the period was, of course, square-headed. Mouldings similar to those surrounding the windows framed the doorway also.

There was little opportunity for a display of Renaissance ornament on the timber frame of a middle-class Elizabethan house. Sometimes, however, there is a Classical cornice—perhaps complete with a 'dentil course'—passing along the line of a jetty in place of the mediaeval 'coving'. Rarely one might find a line of similar cornice capping a doorway or window—but it would be still some time before the village carpenter could acquaint himself with the detail of what was to him still a foreign innovation.

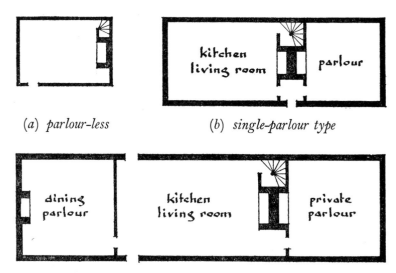

(a) *parlour-less*   (b) *single-parlour type*

(c) *most elaborate type of house having two parlours*

Fig. 8. Seventeenth-century 'long house'. By the close of the century many average-sized houses had two parlours; the uses shown above are conjectural and based on the arrangement found in the Elizabethan great houses. Note how the site of the entrance doorway varies between types (b) and (c)

It has been noted earlier that during the latter years of the sixteenth century the fine timber technique of the south-eastern builders was spreading west and north towards the upper Marches of Wales. When making this advance, the craft of the wrights had necessarily to skip the timberless region of the Cotswold Hills. But farmhouses were wanted there as well, the result being that in the Cotswold region the mediaeval stone-building technique continued as before, but the house plans

78

followed those of the contemporary timber-builders and the details lost much of their old mediaeval style. Thus while Gothic mouldings continued to ornament wooden window frames, the stone-framed windows of the Cotswolds became deprived of their mouldings and restricted to simple chamfers.

The usual central chimney-stack—less elaborate, perhaps, than the contemporary brick stack—was, of course, the principal feature of these houses; they were able, however, to benefit greatly from the skill of the masons by displaying rows of attractive gablets containing windows for lighting the attic storey.

The upper floors of these houses were all framed up with cross-beams and a series of median beams as in their timber counterparts. The cross-beams having no posts to connect as in a timber frame, they were spaced at convenient intervals along the house. Thus the 'bays' of the floor generally bear no relationship to the external elevation of the house; their ends may even be supported on the timber lintels over large windows. As might be expected, the framed floors of these stone-built houses are usually in just as bad a condition today as those in their timber-built brethren.

The stair of a stone-built house was sometimes a properly masoned spiral or humble caracole; more often it was the normal rustic Elizabethan stair of oak treads surrounding a central pole.

While the chimney-stack of the timber-framed house was generally set in the middle of the span, in the case of stone-built houses it was the more frequent practice to set the stack against one of the outer walls and thus economize in material but utilizing this as one side of the chimney opening. (Fig. 9).

It will be appreciated that each era, as well as producing new houses, contributed its own improvements to existing structures. Thus the Tudor era abolished the central hearths and added chimney-stacks set against outer walls. The early seventeenth-century contribution sometimes completed the added unit by combining the stack with an adjunct housing a caracole. 'Trimming' an existing floor might have been too difficult for the builders of the day; thus the typical Elizabethan central unit of stack and stair was added instead to the face of the building. (Fig. 13a).

An interesting style of building appeared at the beginning of the seventeenth century in those regions—such as South Wiltshire—where freestone was only moderately available but the chalk Downs provided plenty of flint nodules. Walls were built there of square stone blocks set alternately on one face and on the one opposite, the 'tail' of each stone being filled up with flints and a face provided of flint nodules cracked in half and set with the black interior showing. This chequerwork walling was very simple to construct, economical of freestone, and to this day looks most attractive (14). The general style of planning and detailing is that of the Cotswold masons.

The sixteenth century saw the ranks of the house-builders —masons and wrights—swelled by the addition of a new craft,

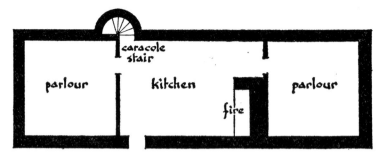

Fig. 9. Typical late-seventeenth or early-eighteenth century rubble-stone farmhouse. In single-parlour type, stairs would be beside fireplace

that of the bricklayer. By the reign of Henry VIII, bricks had been accepted as a suitable material for the construction of the very finest buildings. The small bricks—about two-thirds of the thickness of the modern material—were insufficiently burnt and thus were of a lovely crimson colour; laid in the lime mortar which until comparatively recent times was the only available bedding material, the pattern of white threads on a soft crimson background introduced a warmth and gaiety which a mediaeval stone building could never have achieved.

The art of brick-making came from the Low Countries, whose craftsmen showed us also the unlimited possibilities of moulding and shaping the clay before firing it to any form desired. It is perhaps the 'red masons' of the period when the sixteenth century was turning into the next who were the real exponents of the Renaissance in England. In their endless variations of clustered chimney shafts especially, they translated the Classical colonnette into something of which Vignola would never have approved, but without which the skyline of England would be the poorer today.

The Renaissance door-case took the form of an 'aedicule'—a decorative feature based on a small-scale reproduction of the end of a building or a portico. An 'Order' was, of course, employed, either the plain Doric or the more elaborate Corinthian with its voluted acanthus capital. The columns were flattened into pilasters and joined across their tops by an 'entablature' of architrave, frieze, and cornice; sometimes a triangular 'pediment' completed the aedicule. Any carved ornament was generally of the low-relief type known as arabesque.

The Italian Renaissance was a very long time settling down in England. Contact was by hearsay and an occasional amateur sketch. Thus the turned baluster which was such a feature of Continental architecture at this time became curiously distorted on its arrival in England. For some reason or other it arrived upside down—with the bulge at the top instead of the bottom— and there it stuck fast throughout Elizabethan and Jacobean architecture!

There were no lathes for turning balusters, so the joiners made their balusters square. In any case it was only as balustrades to grand stairs and the occasional ornamental parapet that the baluster appeared; the smaller house had no use for it. But sometimes you may find in small farmhouses of the period a short length of balustrade—as a partition, or at the head of a small rustic staircase—with its balusters cut out of board, in a fretted style which often includes cut-outs of a description not encountered anywhere except in the curious Renaissance forms of the Elizabethan–Jacobean era in England.

Another result of the Renaissance movement was the improvement of interior finishes. The beamed ceiling which formed such a delightful feature of the Tudor parlour began to be covered over with split laths and a plaster of lime and cowhair; only the main beams of the framed floor being allowed to show on the ceiling. Internal wall surfaces—in the great houses covered with tapestry hangings—were in lesser houses plastered over to hide the roughnesses of the masonry or brickwork. (In framed houses, of course, the timbers still showed internally between plastered panels, as on the exterior of the building.)

The last half of the sixteenth century saw a phenomenal development in the art of the plasterer, and the beginning of the next century its zenith when enormously elaborate and massively moulded plaster ceilings were the vogue. The ornamental ceiling remained with us throughout the seventeenth century, becoming consciously Baroque at the time of the Restoration, wandering into the flippancies of the Rococo at the mid-Georgian period, and then settling down into the delicate Classical ceiling designs of the end of the century when the Adam brothers held undisputed sway over the followers of the Classical School.

The internal sheathing of constructional timbering with boarding had been practised during mediaeval times, its earliest use having been to cover over the exposed roof timbering of the open timber roofs above such important positions as the hall dais or the principal bed in the great chamber. As such boarding resembled in contour the tilt of a wagon it was known as 'wainscot'. The use of boarded 'wainscot' was expanded to cover internal wall surfaces to conceal damp penetration. Boarded partitions, too, were of wainscot. The usual form was the 'bratticing' of planks set vertically and spaced apart, with other planks covering the spaces. By the fifteenth century, wainscot had become framed up into panelling as we now know it. At the time of Henry VIII it was in common use in ordinary houses. The panels were small, with only the vertical members being moulded while the horizontal ones remained plain. The panels were often carved with the curious form of moulding known as 'linenfold'. The Elizabethans squared up the panels and left them plain. By the seventeenth century the frame of the panelling was being moulded throughout, with the corners properly mitred.

The Tudor house always had the short 'spur' screen projecting inside the main door of the hall, with usually a similar one to the lesser door opposite. After the movable central screen had been absorbed as a fixture, the completed screen with its pair of doors became the standard finish for the lower end of the hall, dividing this from 'the screens'—as the passage across the hall was known. Sometimes this passage was floored over to provide the 'minstrels' gallery' upon which some rustic orchestra might perform to the delectation of the company in the hall. Even quite small Elizabethan and Jacobean manor houses could boast a hall screen and gallery.

The Elizabethan door followed the same joinery system as the panelling, appearing as a feature divided into square panels by moulded framing. External doors were usually lined with boarding to strengthen them. They were still hung on 'hooks and bands' to their frames of wood, stone, or brick.

A feature which the Elizabethans joyfully retained from their ancestors was the sheltering porch of mediaeval days, which they raised to full height with a small room over as in the church porches of the previous century—this room probably retaining its traditional function of muniment room housing the family records.

A very important innovation of the Renaissance era, accompanying the abolition of Gothic lettering in favour of the more legible Roman, was the introduction of Arabic numerals, in place of the Latin system which had for so long made it impossible for anyone to perform the simplest mathematical function—even ordinary addition—without using a chequer board. The Elizabethans seem to have been greatly taken with the new figures and from the middle of the century onwards proudly exhibited the year of foundation of each house over its front door, a practice followed by their successors for generations to come.

The sixteenth century was a conspiratorial one, with political and religious changes the order of the day. This and the next century was the era of the secret room or hidey-hole, a great number of examples of which may still be seen—and are yet to be discovered—in the houses of the period. The unoccupied spaces adjoining the great Elizabethan chimney-stacks were favourite sites for hidey-holes, and small tucked-away attics were also used. Tiny rooms, and steep stairs to attics, could easily be concealed behind the ubiquitous panelling; only by measuring up a building and drawing up its plan can one detect hollow areas behind the bland inscrutability of cunningly-joinered panelling. It was not even necessary to mask the door —for the hidey-hole could be entered from inside what appeared to be a perfectly innocuous closet.

CHAPTER IV

The Long Houses of the Seventeenth Century

————— ✸ —————

We have seen in the previous chapter how the mediaeval type of house began to die out at the period of the Reformation and became replaced by a rationalized form of structure having a simplified plan more in line with the arrangement of the small house as we know it today. That the Jacobean period saw an awakening interest in housing is demonstrated by local legislative moves towards the abolishment of the home-made hovel. At this time, a house sixteen feet in span and thirty feet long was considered the minimum requirement for a family; moreover a properly-constructed chimney was considered essential and the old open bonfire in the middle of the floor very much frowned on by local authority. And there can be no doubt that the new rationalized house-form had come to stay; indeed, during the seventeenth century these standardized houses became distributed throughout the whole country, to form the substance of our domestic architecture—as it still exists, in village and country town, to this present day (Fig. 8).

While adhering rigidly to their fundamental plan-forms, the long houses varied considerably in size as well as, of course, in structural quality. They could be based on spans of sixteen, twenty or twenty-four feet in width, with corresponding variations in length of building bay. They could have walling only one storey in height with the whole of the chamber floor within the roof and perhaps two or three gablets set along the main elevation for lighting purposes, while the finest among them

84

13. Typical eighteenth-century domestic architecture of the rural south-east of England. Sash-windowed bays are beginning to replace the leaded lights in iron casements still to be seen in the timber-framed, tile-hung upper storey. A tile-roofed 'Sussex hip' closes this vista of house-fronts at Groombridge in Kent.

14. Rural building technique at Broadchalke in Wiltshire. The mid-seventeenth century portion has a typical mullioned window with a label mould over, set in a chequerwork of freestone blocks alternating with flint panels. The late-eighteenth-century window has a flat arch of rubbed bricks; the walling above is in 'garden wall bond' with two rows of stretchers to every row of headers. The thatch is West Country straw reed.

might have an additional attic storey above the main chamber floor.

The early seventeenth century was the period of the greatest development of the masonry style of the Cotswolds, a stone-building region which, at one time of small importance, had come into its own with the development of the wool trade. All the pleasant tricks of Jacobean building—the central stack, the tall porch, the gablets along the roof, were indulged in to produce an architectural style which never fails to delight us.

The timber-builders were still hard at work in their own districts. Jetties had gone for ever and the rather exiguous, sprawling, tall 'balloon' frames which rose from footing to roof-plate had now become the standard practice (12). A shortage of timber could easily be detected in the manner in which small timbers were used; the decay of craftsmanship could be seen in the absence of any attempt to create a pattern in the timbering. The large panels were now being filled, in addition to the older materials, with broken brick-bats. Inside, the badly-designed framed floors were already cracking at the joints. The central stack, still lording it over the whole building, had become a plain square lump containing the flues (7).

But the house-wrights were on their way out. Taking their place as the most important building craftsmen of the day were the bricklayers—the 'red masons' who had replaced the free-masons of mediaeval times.

The bricklayers had become a very important section of the building trade. For where no field-stone existed for building chimney-stacks, the only possible way of providing yourself with one of the great stacks which had become the all-essential feature of a house was to obtain the services of a bricklayer.

The brick-waller was now as much a part of the house-building fraternity as had been the stone-waller or the house-wright with his timber frames. The technique of laying bricks in an orderly fashion so as to produce a strong 'bond' was now properly understood. The thin two-inch bricks of Tudor days had been laid anyhow as long as the wall was not weakened by vertical 'straight joints'. But the Elizabethan builders had devised the system known as 'English Bond' which consists in laying alternate courses of 'stretchers'—bricks running along the wall-face—and 'headers' which are bricks set at right-angles to this. But most bricklaying technique was learnt from the original source of supply—the Low Countries—and by the end of the seventeenth century English builders were using the 'Flemish Bond' which consists of laying each course in alternating headers and stretchers and setting the headers and stretchers alternately above each other. Thereafter the Continental system superseded the English in so far as face brickwork was concerned.

The framed walling of farmhouses was now being superseded everywhere by walls of brickwork. It is interesting to note, however, that the bricklayers were not too sure of their ability to raise walls of too great a height; thus it is not uncommon to see the brick walling stop at eaves level and the gables constructed in timber framing tying up with the roof timbering.

Once jetties have been abandoned, and the curious top-heavy silhouette of mediaeval days vanishes from the scene, the house adopts a form indistinguishable from that of today. The two-storied 'balloon' frame may be subsequently disguised by sheathing it with lath-and-plaster or even by encasing the whole frame in walls of brick or stone. But the existence of the frame within is nearly always disclosed by the thickening-out of the tops of the tall posts to take the joints of the beams entering them at roof level. These seventeenth-century 'teazle-heads' are always internal and thus may often be seen projecting from a plastered wall which might otherwise give no indication of being in fact a timber frame.

The same Elizabethan standard plan of kitchen-living-room and parlour, separated by the great stack and having above them chambers and attics, was being followed. But the windows had become plain frames of squared timber set into the walls, with hand-wrought iron casements hung on hooks for opening lights. The door-frames were also just massive constructions of plain squared timber.

Inside were the clumsy framed floors. The main beams of these had now to rest on thin brick walls; thus in order to give the end of each beam an adequate bearing on the wall but not expose its end grain to the entry of water, a brick 'string course' about four courses high was run all round the building just below first floor level. These string courses are ubiquitous features of all seventeenth-century brick buildings.

To provide as much space as possible in the attic, the 'roof trusses' were abolished and a dreadfully inefficient system was devised of framing up the roof timbers in the same way as those of the floor below. The purlins were tenoned into the principal rafters, seriously weakening these. Fortunately for the peace of mind of house-owners, a great number of seventeenth-century roofs have long ago been replaced.

As the last traces of mediaeval architecture vanished from even the smallest houses, Renaissance features began to creep in to take their place. Since the very inception of the stone wall, it had been absolutely necessary to provide the large dressed stones called 'quoins' at all external angles. Hitherto these quoins had been for practical use only, varying in size, and lining up with the wall-face. A feature of Renaissance architecture was the selection of quoin stones of standard sizes so that a regular pattern would be formed at the angles. This was especially desirable where the walling was of brick and the white stone angles of the building showed up prominently.

A development of this device was to project the quoins slightly in advance of the wall face; this emphasized the pattern where the wall was of stone. The bricklayer was soon copying this arrangement in his own material by forming artificial quoins in brickwork and giving these the same projection. This notable Renaissance feature of the 'rusticated' angle develops throughout the seventeenth century and at its close is appearing in quite small buildings.

The Renaissance having been firmly established in the minds of architects, the better-class houses were being provided with tall windows having a height of twice their width—the normal Renaissance proportion. The windows were two lights wide with a central mullion; the necessity of dividing up the height of each light into two forced the builders to introduce a horizontal transom which divided the window into four lights. These cruciform windows were typical of the seventeenth century, but so many of them had their mullions and transoms removed during the following century, in order to insert the popular sliding sashes, that there are very few of them remaining today. The lights were glazed with leaded glass and the lower pair were opening iron casements. From henceforth the tall Renaissance window is a mark of housing status; only the very humble

87

were content with the low mullioned type of window, having indeed to continue with them long after the sash window had replaced the hinged casement.

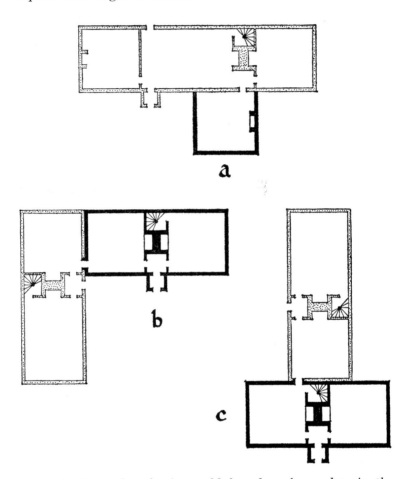

Fig. 10. Examples of wings added to long houses late in the seventeenth century or early in the eighteenth ((c) remains popular, with modifications, throughout the eighteenth century)

It is interesting to see the gradual change in the attitude towards windows which accompanied the transition from the mediaeval to the Renaissance. Hitherto the ordinary householder had found them a nuisance, letting in wind and rain, expensive to glaze, and affording entry to robbers. Nobody needed light to read by, and when the sun shone it was time to be out of doors.

The Black Death, starting in Dorset and sweeping thence throughout the country, had confirmed everyone's belief that plague was borne on the south wind. Thus houses were wherever possible set north and south so as to present a narrow windowless end towards the pestilence. Even where village streets ran east and west their houses were often set at right-angles to them.

It may have been the increase in scholarship accompanying the Renaissance which brought the daylight into English houses, expanding their windows and setting new wings across southern gables so as to turn a new face towards the sunshine.

Improvement of the brick supply brought with it the increased use of clay tiles for roofing. Tiles can be used to finish a gable—the edge of tiling at this point is known as the 'verge'— far more efficiently than thatch. The gabled end is therefore a common feature of seventeenth-century England; very often a chimney stack is incorporated with the gable. The tiling looks tidier when finished against a parapet instead of as a verge; the best houses therefore show parapeted gables even where the main walls overhang as eaves.

At this period the Low Countries were sending over a large number of interlocking tiles of a new type. Based on a modification of the Spanish tile, which is a hollow tile laid alternately with the hollow up and down, these wavy 'pantiles' may be seen in large quantities on the seventeenth-century roofs of East Anglia. They make poor verges, so that the parapeted gable end is almost universal in those parts, contrasting with the ordinary plain-tiled verge to the south-east and south.

A feature only met with on the eastern side of England is the so-called 'Dutch' gable with the wavy Baroque silhouette which was devised originally in Spain and reached us via the Low Countries. In the country of their origin and its colonies they were of stone or were plastered; in England they were left in brick, sometimes pleasantly embellished with fancy brickwork.

Throughout the seventeenth century the rural housewright continued to raise his timber frames. The incorporation of the roof space within the accommodation (in the case of the humbler type of house the whole of the chamber storey might be in the roof) necessitated the use of the gabled end for lighting purposes. Constructed in lengths of timber, the gable itself was always apt to be a weak spot on the frame; it might even become detached from the timbering below and fall outwards. Thus one frequently finds the pair of crucks—the traditional 'gable-fork'—introduced into the gable end to serve as a rigid, properly triangulated, foundation for the tall structure. Most of the crucks one sees today are of seventeenth-century origin. Broadly speaking, one can say that the bent or "knee" cruck is later than the arched form and represents the ultimate development of this interesting and striking feature.

The history of the middle-class house or farmhouse is frequently one of copyism—the aping of the squire's house by the yeoman. An essential apartment in the Elizabethan mansion was the winter parlour which was the ancestor of our dining-room. We therefore find that some of the larger seventeenth-century farmhouses, especially in the south and east, had a parlour at the lower end of the living-room kitchen as well as at the end next the great stack. (Fig. 8c). To heat this parlour it was usual to build a small stack passing up the gable end of the building, a situation from which it was eventually to oust the great central feature. The long two-parloured houses, with their central and lesser stacks, are very much a product of the seventeenth century; they are found in considerable numbers in the Cotswold region. The entrance is very occasionally next the great stack, as in the single-parlour houses, but more often in the traditional place at the lower end of the hall—now the kitchen-living-room ((10) Fig. 8c).

The existence of a number of parlours in a house of the seventeenth century does not necessarily mean that their use was entirely restricted to social purposes. Indeed it is known that they were often used as overflow bedrooms to accommodate a large family or at times of hospitality. Only the principal room itself remained inviolate as a centre of social life.

Even in mansion houses the custom of dining in feudal state in one's great hall died out at the end of the Civil War. Apart from the accepted inconvenience to those seated at the high table which had led to the introduction of the winter parlour, the Puritan attitude to communal dining in hall seems to have been to regard it as a sort of public orgy. The farmhouse, however, was still in its degree a feudal structure and communal eating in its great kitchen an essential feature of rural life. Thus the farmhouse kitchen of the seventeenth century retained something of the nature of its noble predecessor and the culinary operations carried out at its cavernous fireplace formed only a minor feature of its activities.

The fundamental factor governing the ordinance of any mediaeval house-plan is the insistence upon keeping a firm distinction between the 'upper' and 'lower' ends of the building. Thus the parlour, with its 'chamber of estate' over, was often given special treatment; it was sometimes constructed in more permanent materials or had special architectural treatment. Any expansion of the house's living accommodation would probably be added to its parlour end.

The lower end of the house was usually that adjoining the working area of the farmyard. In the smaller holdings, a barn or byre often forms part of the building itself and is included under the one roof. Such an appendage may occasionally be converted into living accommodation. Conversions of this sort were not, however, a feature in early domestic planning; indeed the whole principle of 'conversion', first employed on a large scale when the farmhouses were broken up during the Enclosure Era, is very much a modern device, a makeshift seldom employed by the old builder who preferred to plan from the outset.

Within the house the fireplace of the second half of the seventeenth century showed a marked change from the mediaeval type which had been employed up-to-date. The opening was now, in deference to Renaissance feeling, square-headed; the 'architrave' moulding often surrounded the whole feature to give it a frame. Its interior was neatly constructed and protected by a fireback, and, as coal was now coming into use as fuel, there was often some sort of basket device available for holding it. The overmantels of the Elizabethan Age were sometimes replaced by a simple moulded frame in the form of a large panel. In fine houses there was sometimes a frame of carved ornament, elaborate in its execution but restricted within orderly lines.

The farmhouse kitchen-living-room was always given a capacious fireplace for log-burning, equipped with all the various devices to help in cooking for a large number of farm hands. These took their meals while seated at one or two refectory-type tables set at the 'lower' or door end of the room. The farmer himself had his 'gate-leg' table drawn out from the wall, opened up, and set in front of the fire for himself and his family.

The back of the fireplace, which forms the base of the heavy chimney-stack itself, was usually of some thickness and in it was formed the baking oven provided with its cast-iron door. It was heated at night by burning heather in it or by filling it with embers from the fire which were raked out in the morning and the hot cavern used for baking bread and pies.

The front of the fireplace was flanked by strong supports of stone or brick carrying the sturdy chimney beam from which the capacious chimney flue was gathered back. Behind these supports, the sides of the more spacious fireplaces were often recessed to provide shelving or even seats; arm rests and a niche for salt may sometimes be found cut in the thick rear wall of the fireplace.

The chimney-stack of the period had lost its elaborate Jacobean shafting and was now a massive structure, either square or cruciform on plan with the flues concealed within. The chimney cap was generally a brickwork version of a Classical entablature, each moulding being represented by a projecting course of bricks.

We have now watched the mediaeval buildings of England developing towards the magnificence of the Tudor Era with its glorious banqueting halls and its forests of chimneys fretting the skyline. Yet within a century all this magnificence had already become anachronistic. The Middle Ages had ended— the Renaissance not yet arrived. The dismal transition period of the seventeenth century had the country in its grip.

With the passing of the great Queen much of the spirit seemed to go out of England. Her reign was the last fling of mediaeval pageantry; with her humourless successor appeared an era of drabness. The mediaeval Church, struggling to survive, only plunged the nation into the misery of political strife—the savagery of judicial murders in the course of which great men such as Raleigh, the Archbishop of Canterbury, and finally, to the horror of Europe, the King of England himself, were decapitated. Englishmen clubbed each other to death on

15. The Cotswold builders of the seventeenth century often made a special feature of the chamber gable at the upper end of the house. During the third quarter of the century they designed most attractive house-fronts having a pair of such gables linked by a porch. Stone-mullion construction enabled wide windows to be spanned with ease, the parlour window of this house at Stanton in Gloucestershire being a good example of the period.

16. A late seventeenth-century farmhouse at Broadway in Worcestershire with the chambers in its attic storey lit by dormer windows instead of the earlier gablets. It has been divided up into cottages during the 'Enclosure' period of the close of the eighteenth or beginning of the nineteenth century, when the little bay windows were added.

the battlefields of the Civil War; the wounded and dead were stripped by wretched peasantry still living in mediaeval squalor in their home-made hovels.

But religious superstition and the romance of chivalry was losing the field to a new ideal—that of scholarship. The introduction of Arabic numerals made arithmetical calculation for the first time possible. Printing had become well established and, now that Roman type founts had replaced Gothic blackletter, learning could be more easily spread through the medium of books. The colonels of the Civil War planned their campaigns not only with the help of amazingly accurate maps of England but even had printed road books of the principal routes to assist them. The roads themselves were still merely routes between towns, neither engineered nor metalled—but for year after year the armies trudged along them, horse and foot, cannon and wagon train, and they became well known to many Englishmen who had never left their villages before.

Thus the Civil War of the middle of the century had a notable effect upon the transport system of England. The wagon-trains of cheeses and cannon balls were followed by huge transport wagons of merchandise tugged by powerful teams along the rutted or miry routes. The second half of the seventeenth century is the Wagon Age. The villages became transformed as new by-passes came into use, skirting the hovel-flanked lane which had been the village street, or thrusting into, and away from, the village green of mediaeval times. As there was no metalling these wagon routes had to be wide enough to allow navigators to pick their way; these wide thoroughfares of the late seventeenth century became the spacious High Streets of Georgian days.

And with the wagons came loads of the new building material —bricks. No longer were provincial builders dependent upon the country's forests for the substance of their houses. Even to the clayless regions, bricks could now be imported by wagon. The Elizabethans had shown in their mansions what could be done with bricks; now they had become a commercial proposition for the middle-class builder.

The Dissolution of the Monasteries had seen the destruction of the ecclesiastical glories of England. The defeat of the upper classes at the end of the Civil War completed the revolution.

The Long Houses of the Seventeenth Century

As with the great monastic houses, now it was the turn of the proud castles with their many palatial interiors to be given over to the attentions of the miner with his galleries, his props, and his devouring fires. Not only strong towers, but great halls and noble houses tumbled into ruin and were exposed to the inspection of the ordinary man. Here was a fresh source of building material and, moreover, yet another chance, to those who might be interested, of further investigation into the problems of building science relative to the erection of fine buildings.

The aesthetic revolution of the Italian Renaissance had begun to reach England—in a much confused condition—during the sixteenth century. But England's real Renaissance was the intellectual one of post-Civil War days. The pageantry of the Elizabethan Era had been but an extension of mediaeval pomp. After the wretched years of the Puritan reformation, culminating in the shameful war with its aftermath of ignorant demagoguery, the cheerful era of the Restoration restored the spirit of the country and re-created it, purged at last of all traces of mediaevalism, as a modern nation on the road to world leadership.

The foundation of 'The Royal Society for Improving Natural Knowledge' (1662) demonstrated that there was a new scholarship abroad, an interest in phenomena which could be studied on their merits and without fear of interference from interested bodies such as the mediaeval Church. It was the age of Newton and his discoveries. The builder who wished to keep up-to-date in his technique had to abandon the practices of centuries and familiarize himself with the latest views on current building science. In 1668 the first of a series of textbooks on building was published—these publications, of which the best known, Moxon's, went into many editions, provided illustrations of details which could now be learned from study rather than as heretofore by mere copying.

During the seventeenth century the long houses were spreading throughout the south and east of England. They are especially ubiquitous in the wool-rich and brick-producing countryside of East Anglia—a land of towering brick chimney-clusters bestriding long roof-lines (8). But it was these same impressive features—fearful obstructions in the very heart of

94

the building—which doomed the long house to become abandoned after little more than a century of popularity. Moreover, it was found that it had been only an excursion into domestic architecture and we are now to realize that it played no part in the direct historical line.

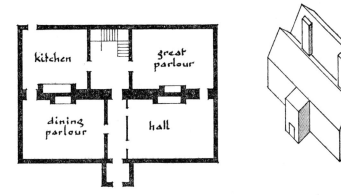

(*a*) *early-seventeenth-century form having pair of single-span roofs*

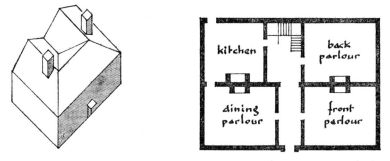

(*b*) *late-seventeenth-century form having double-span roof and hip*

Fig. 11. Development of Renaissance manor-farmhouse
(*see also Figs. 4 and 12*)

The long house with the central stack had been a notable experiment. But in the end it was the humble Tudor house which survived—'underground' as it were—to re-emerge in the eighteenth century as the Georgian cottage (Figs. 13 and 14). And at the other end of the scale, the upper-class 'manorial' type of structure was developing along its own lines (Figs. 11

95

and 12) without concerning itself with the standardized experimental architecture of the middle classes. Let us therefore return to consider the seventeenth century in the light of its accumulated discoveries in building science.

One feature of mediaeval building which was long in dying out was the 'single-span' system of construction. This simply means that all buildings were constructed to be covered by a single roof-tree, extension being either by prolongating this or by building another single-span construction at right-angles to the original in the manner of a wing. Thus every roof discharged its storm-water down to eaves, either dripping or provided with some kind of eaves gutter.

The two-storied house often had its roof extended downwards at the rear of the building to cover small rooms of storeroom type added there. This addition to the main structure was known as the 'outshot' (Fig. 13b); any single-storey addition covered with a lean-to roof became known by the same designation. Masons' 'lodges', built against the walls of the structure they were erecting, were outshots—the two words were often used synonymously.

The humble lodge, such as, for instance, that which in Georgian days and after housed the gatekeeper of the great house, should not be confused with the hunting lodge. This has existed since Tudor times, having been a large house erected by the Warden of a forest region to provide seasonal lodgings for persons engaging in the sport of venery.

The outshot was popular during the seventeenth century and most small houses of the period were provided with these additions for use as pantries or wash-houses. In this way it was possible to increase the area of at least the ground floor of the building.

By raising the outshot to two storeys in height and thus setting two complete single-span buildings side by side, the builders faced a serious problem—what to do with the storm-water in the valley between the roofs. The great buildings of the Middle Ages had been provided with parapets—often highly decorative features—instead of the primitive eaves. This had necessitated the construction of gutters behind the parapet to collect the water from the roof and lead it to spouting gargoyles. The construction of these gutters had been a difficult exercise in carpentry and plumbing, for a gutter must be watertight and even the builders of today are well aware that a gutter of this sort has to be very scientifically constructed if it is to fulfil its task. But above all, a parapet gutter cannot be constructed without using lead, and lead in mediaeval days was expensive and plumbers to work it almost entirely monopolized by the ecclesiastical authorities.

The Reformation changed all that. The Dissolution of the Monasteries released enormous quantities of lead (after the land itself the most valuable spoil of the campaign) and the plumbers were, of course, quick in following their material. Not only were the great houses able to be parapeted about in an orderly fashion, but the plumbers were able if required to provide valley gutters between adjoining single-span roofs.

This resulted in a revolution in planning. No longer had buildings to be planned in single spans and thus only one room in thickness. Before the sixteenth century was out, John Thorpe and his colleagues were designing mansions two rooms in thickness, the hall no longer lit on both sides but with windows on the main front and apartments adjoining on the other side (Fig. 11a).

It was the introduction of the double-span plan which furthered the development of the central stack for heating rooms on either side of it. With plenty of lead now available it was no very difficult matter for the plumbers to take the stacks up through the valley and still keep the construction watertight with 'flashings'. In the case of the standard type of farmhouse which developed as the result of the invention of the central stack, this came up through the ridge and could be made watertight quite simply, even without the use of lead.

The earliest double-span houses were those having as it were an 'outshot' which had been rebuilt to the same height as the main portion of the building and like it covered with an ordinary pitched roof (Fig. 11a). But eventually the often waterlogged valley disappeared and the whole house became covered with a single, heavily-timbered roof of very wide span. In order to avoid having monstrously ill-proportioned gables at the ends of the building, the roof was carried across these by means of sloping 'hips'. Such roofs were not at all easy to construct; at first the lateral roofs were taken back as if they covered wings, which again left a valley gutter, albeit much shorter, between them (Fig. 11b). Sometimes the roof was hipped all round to leave a depression in the middle which had to be provided with a 'secret gutter' to carry the rainwater away from it through an attic. But eventually the use of lead enabled the Georgian builders to cover over this depression with a 'lead flat' (Fig. 12).

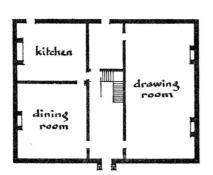
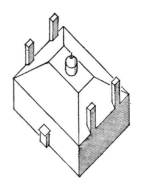

Fig. 12. Georgian house-plan (see also Fig. 11)
(Kitchen and its offices are often set in semi-basement
below main floor)

The plan of the larger or 'manorial' type of farmhouse develops independently of the essentially single-span 'long houses'. Under their broad hipped roofs the 'square' Renaissance houses accept the principle of the Elizabethan chimney stack by setting it between pairs of front and back rooms with the chimneys emerging through the hipped ends of the roof (Fig. 11b); during the eighteenth century the external chimney-stack of the Georgians replaces the internal Elizabethan form (Fig. 12). By this time the neat hipped roof, saved from becoming oppressive by the dormer windows lighting the attic within it, has become the normal form of covering for a small English house.

Thus we see the planning ordinances of the whole country turning away from the single-span building having a very definite long axis, towards the squarer type of structure with a second dimension beginning to approach the first. The end of a mediaeval building had been simply a gable end, whereas the end of a building of the seventeenth century might have a definite 'end elevation', not only requiring careful architectural treatment but perhaps even having to be brought into line with the longer elevations adjoining it.

The small houses of the Elizabethan Age could have a wing or two added if required. A century later, however, some attempt would be made to fit the accommodation required into the space outlined by the main walls of the building. The old hall or kitchen-living-room could no longer survive as a large room forming the nucleus of the house, it had now become merely one of the units—albeit still the most important—making up the house plan. Parlours and a staircase had to be fitted in as well, with chambers and attics above.

In mediaeval times, the upper storey of a house containing the sleeping accommodation was not considered as requiring anything in the way of a monumental approach. But the introduction of the Elizabethan long gallery had suddenly brought the upper part of the house into social prominence; hence the emergence of the fine staircase in its special tower. Early in the seventeenth century the Renaissance *piano nobile* appears in impressive form when the planning unit represented by the reduced Great Hall is echoed on the storey above by a magnificent apartment which is in fact the re-sited Great Parlour. Usually dignified by a large and elaborately ornamented chimneypiece, this elevated parlour is a forerunner, though perhaps hardly a true ancestor—for it failed to survive the Civil War—of the drawing-room of Georgian days.

The corridor for circulation within a house is a very late invention; the finest Jacobean mansions had their rooms entered one from another. The corridor may have first developed as an extension of the lobby which was sometimes contrived at the end of a small closet or dressing-room separating two large apartments. A planning device introduced during the Restoration period to 'square up' the mansion plan was to double the spinal wall separating the back and front rooms and provide a narrow passage between them. The same device is found in some of the finer Georgian houses; on the whole, however, it was the central staircase hall which provided circulation between rooms the more remote of which had to be reached in the traditional manner.

As architectural skill developed, the designers took a preconceived rectangle as their planning basis and fitted the various rooms within the bounds of this. As time went on they adopted the orderly system of elevational design which had been for some time followed, Renaissance fashion, by the architects working on large mansions. With first the front, then the rear, and then the now greatly extended lateral elevations to tackle in this fashion, they found themselves in the end up against problems often greater in magnitude, because smaller in scale, than those faced by the designers of the great houses of the land.

The fascinating feature of the whole situation is that the designers of these smaller farmhouses and middle-class homes were generally not architects at all, but merely the actual builders themselves who, armed with textbooks to help them, took sufficient pride in their craft to rejoice their clients with buildings as aesthetically complete in their way as anything produced by the fashionable architects of the day.

This is a fact which should be remembered. The architect of today was represented in the past by the builder himself, the mansion-builder alone being excepted. All the beautifully-designed farmhouses and smaller homes of the past three centuries are the product of the local builder with his well-thumbed textbook and his traditional pride in his craft to guide him in his achievements.

Probably the most important influence upon seventeenth-century building technique in this country was that of the brick-layer, travelling with his material from its sources, settling wherever new supplies of clay could be turned to his use, and owing nothing to the anachronistic art of the stonemason. He could be relied upon to be familiar with the most recent building methods and his handy and easily manipulated bricks had an apparently endless variety of uses.

It was during the seventeenth century that the oaken lintel for spanning door and window openings began to give place to the brick arch.

Bricks were a great boon to the builders in the chalk regions where flint nodules had long been the principal building material.

17. Late-seventeenth-century farmhouses at Wherwell in Hampshire which have been divided into cottages. We can see that the day of the house-wrights is drawing near its close, yet the clumsily-constructed timber frames have managed to hold together for close on three centuries and will doubtless continue to do so for many years yet.

18. In the more sophisticated regions of England the cottages of the eighteenth century were built by landowners employing professional builders. These Cornish cottages at Boscastle suggest that the local fishermen may have helped each other to raise their rustic homes of rubble stone and local slate.

No longer had the waller to obtain freestone for quoins and the 'dressings' round openings. (A delightful feature of flint houses of the eighteenth century is the brick 'lacing course' set across the house fronts and joining quoin to quoin.)

The seventeenth-century towns of England were still mediaeval, with narrow alleys, narrow frontages, and tall skyscrapers still almost entirely of jettied timberwork. Only the capital and a few of the more important cities were beginning to reface their old buildings with brick frontispieces replacing the timber frames, steadying to some extent the jumble of timberwork, letting some light into the dark mediaeval canyons, and lessening the fire-risk.

The appearance of the mediaeval street frontage had been regulated by the narrow widths—sixteen to twenty feet—of the frontages, and also the custom of using the party walls to support the roof so that a gable always faced the street. The widening of frontages by coupling two or more plots together enabled the long seventeenth-century type of building to be erected on urban sites. Thus from this time onwards the gable begins to disappear from street frontages to be replaced by long elevations capped by eaves or cornices. This type of urban elevation is particularly noticeable in the inns of the Georgian period with their frontages long enough to provide for a wide opening leading to the stable yard behind.

But a modern type of town house was now badly needed. There had been no development of the city merchant's house comparable with that of his rural contemporary. The great town houses of Tudor days had all fallen into decrepitude and either been swept away or become bandit-infested warrens of tenements. There had been no successors, for the Court had been scattered during the Rebellion and had never been revived in its former magnificence. The English nobleman was still for all practical purposes a countryman.

So there was no foundation upon which to develop a modern type of town house in this country. The solution was to investigate the problem as it had been resolved on the Continent, long brought into line with contemporary architectural development following the spread of the Italian Renaissance. The half-timber skyscraper had never appeared in Italy and many regions of France had lacked the timber for its construction.

Thus urban development had been along more orthodox lines with stone walling and plain, tidily-designed, Renaissance house-fronts. This was clearly the type of town house to be introduced into England.

But insular England could never have accepted such a revolutionary innovation without considerable pressure. No existing sites were yet available for reconstruction projects. So the new type of house had to be introduced by an outsider, on a virgin site, and as a speculation. The first of the race of speculative builders was an ex-Commonwealth parliamentarian who, born Barebones but now calling himself Barbon, obtained from the Duke of Bedford, on long lease, land in North London, divided it into building lots, and set himself up as the first estate developer.

His houses were of Continental type, set side by side on narrow frontages in the style of the Italian 'terrace'. They were built of brick and had the usual plain elevations of the Renaissance street frontage. At the side of each house a narrow stair hall ran from front to back; a median wall divided up the remainder of the building so as to provide a pair of rooms on each of its four floors.

The stair itself was of a new type, derived from the square tower stair but having only two parallel flights to each storey separated by a half landing instead of three flights and two quarter landings as in the larger Elizabethan stairs. The 'newel posts' of these had by now become shortened so as to become separate posts at each landing, the top of each post being elaborated with carved detail to produce a magnificent ornamental feature.

The stair of the 'terrace' house had its two flights set parallel to each other. It was known until recent times as a 'pair of stairs' but is now generally called a 'dog-leg stair'. Compact and space-saving in its layout it became by common consent the stair of the future; speedily ousting the various spiral conceptions of other days it has continued in use to modern times.

The stair of the Commonwealth period had been a magnificent example of joinery. Its newels were finished off with robustly carved finials. Wood-turning lathes were now in existence but the true Renaissance baluster—whichever way up—seems to have been somewhat neglected and the turners

102

produced their own versions of delightfully bulgy balusters owing nothing to Michelangelo. This is an interesting example of how a new craft will develop with enthusiasm by making its own experiments rather than by copying the efforts of some earlier exponent of the art.

One of the problems facing the builder of the terrace house was how to light the narrow stair hall at ground-floor level where most of the front wall was taken up by the entrance doorway. The solution was to fill in the space between the doorhead and the brick arch of the opening with a semicircular window; the leadwork holding its glazing being generally set radially, the designation of 'fanlight' was obviously appropriate. Even when the whole door opening was raised, and the fanlight became square in elevation, it still retained its original name.

The invention of the age had been undoubtedly the 'pair of stairs'; that of the previous era the central chimney-stack with its system of fireplaces heating a series of rooms. The time had now come when every house needed either one or both of these conveniences.

The jettied houses were unfitted for improvement as no cutting of their floor joists was possible without the upper part of the house, supported as it was upon their ends, collapsing. But floors had to be cut for the insertion of internal features, so the time was ripe for the obliteration of the jetty by building up brick walls to the ground storey and picking up the timber framework of the upper storey on these. Freed from their task of carrying the frames, the floor joists could now be cut and 'trimmed' to provide a well for stack or stairs.

There are thus many old houses in England which show today in their upper storey the close-set timbering of Tudor times above a ground storey of simple brickwork. Inside you will find the original floor joists disfigured by notches which once held the top member of the ground-floor frame, removed when the later brick walling was built so as to enlarge the ground storey to the same size as the one over.

A fundamental factor in the design of the mediaeval house is the employment of the bay system in which the house is divided at bay interval by transverse beams joining posts in the long outer walls. Mediaeval floor joists were laid either across the building from side to side or longitudinally across large transverse beams. The campaign against waste of timber which accompanied the Spanish threat of the latter part of the sixteenth century resulted in the introduction of a beam passing down the centre of the house so that the floor joists could be

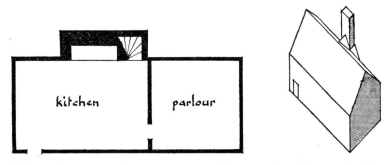

(*a*) *early-seventeenth century type with caracole stair contrived in chimney stack*

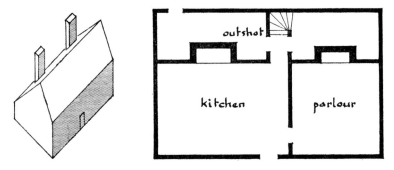

(*b*) *late-seventeenth century type with stair in 'outshot' (chimney stacks later moved to end walls)*

Fig. 13. *Development of humbler class of farmhouse during seventeenth century*

halved in length and thus reduced in size. The extremely rickety construction produced by tenoning the spinal beam into the cross beams eventually resulted in abandoning the latter and concentrating on the former by making it heavier and giving it firm intermediate supports.

The Long Houses of the Seventeenth Century

From the seventeenth century onwards the single large beam having short floor joists 'housed' into its flanks is the standard method of supporting the upper floor. Ceilings were constructed in the same way; as their timbers could not be seen they were left rough and unsquared (often to the dismay of their current owners who are shocked at their rickety appearance and find it difficult to believe that they have been like that for centuries). The halving of the span made it possible to lighten all joists considerably; thus from the broad beams of mediaeval days they change by the seventeenth century to an almost square section.

A great many of these old floors and ceilings have been taken out and replaced with modern ones having softwood joists spanning right across the room without recourse to a great central beam. One may see the salvaged beams—'summers' the old builders called them—lying about all over rural England, either piled in yards to rot or sometimes utilized for fake chimney beams and other 'olde-worlde' features. They may be readily recognized by the slotted 'housings' for their vanished floor joists appearing at regular intervals along their sides. The presence of such reused timbers in old houses often leads people to imagine that they are 'ship's timbers' (the *Mayflower* not excepted!) whereas, of course, all such are curved and totally unsuited to house-building.

The curious system of laying floor joists on their sides and thus greatly reducing their strength and increasing their whippiness had to be abandoned when a shortage of native timber was countered by importing material from Scandinavia. The new timber was softwood, easier to work, less temperamental in its tendency to warp than the English oak, but far weaker in its resistance to loads. Such timber could never have been laid on its side, but the scientific progress of the seventeenth century had enabled the discovery to be made that timber laid on edge would carry a much greater load. Thus from the days of Wren onwards we find the side-laid oaken floor joists giving place to the imported softwood 'deals' laid, in modern fashion, on their edges.

Softwood joists being deemed unsuited to exposure within the room, it became customary to conceal them with lath and plaster, thus obliterating the 'oak-beamed' effect which had

105

hitherto provided the inevitable ceiling treatment in an English parlour. Even though imported softwood remained expensive and rural builders continued for a hundred years or more to use local timber, the plaster ceiling became henceforth used to cover everything up. This resulted in a gradual deterioration in the once sturdy house-carpentry of England, especially with regard to ceilings and even to floors. The nadir was reached during the second quarter of the nineteenth century—presumably as a result of the Napoleonic blockade—when houses of the period may be found to have floors and ceilings made up of all sorts of odd lengths of timber, some of them even set *diagonally* . . . the whole, of course, conveniently concealed behind the ceiling plaster.

But—as has so often happened—constructional slackness was accompanied by fascinating innovations in elevational design. By the end of the seventeenth century the entrance doorway had become established as a determinedly elaborate focus to the design. The projecting 'door-hood' supported on finely-carved 'console' brackets, becomes fashionable and helps in some degree to make up for the loss of the sheltering porches of mediaeval days. With the improvement of lathes, however, it soon became possible to provide proper Renaissance porches having their roofs supported on Classical columns.

During the last quarter of the seventeenth century one long-established feature of English architecture began to disappear from the scene: the mediaeval window glazing of diamond-shaped 'quarries', in leaded 'calms'. This was due to the introduction, probably from the Low Countries, of the sliding window or 'sash' (from the French *chassis*).

These sashes were of wood and were divided up into glazing panels or 'panes' by wooden 'glazing bars' in which the glass was set. At first each window had one fixed sash and one which could be opened by sliding it from side to side in a groove. Later the 'box frame' was introduced; this was a hollow frame of boards containing counterweights by means of which the sashes could be slid up and down. This box frame was taken up by English builders as providing a window of proportions ideally suitable to the ordinary Renaissance window opening. By the middle of the eighteenth century few of the old cruciform windows remained, having been replaced by boxed sashes. It is often possible to detect where this alteration has been made as the top of the window opening sometimes dropped a bit after the old solid frame had been removed.

After the invention of sheet glass capable of being rolled in large sheets had rendered the glazing bar of Georgian days unnecessary, many of the old sash windows lost their pattern of panes, so attractive to look at but so difficult to keep clean. Today even the most devoted admirer of the Georgian style may hesitate before restoring to ravished sashes the original panes without which the house front loses so much of its original charm (8).

During the seventeenth century, the attic storey in the roof came more and more into use. The small gablets containing windows, which were the earlier method of lighting attic rooms, gradually disappeared during the course of the century in favour of the continental 'dormer' window—an opening trimmed between the roof rafters, fitted with a window-frame, and completed with 'cheeks' and a roof (16).

From the Restoration period onwards, the dormer window becomes an important feature in house design, adding considerably to the interest of the exterior of the building. The windows are nearly always two-light, with one half opening as a wrought-iron casement; the glazing is, of course, leaded quarries.

The first dormer roofs were pointed roofs of traditional type. But with the tendency towards abolishing mediaeval forms and replacing them with more severe horizontal lines which is seen at the close of the century, the builders made use of lead to provide dormers with flat roofs which could be finished with a little Renaissance cornice moulding. This is the normal form of the dormer window from now on.

The experimental methods by which English domestic architecture of the seventeenth century was developing were limited to those regions, once the provinces of the wrights, which were now the stamping ground of the bricklayer. In the traditional masonry region of the stone belt which stretched across the country from Somerset to Northamptonshire, building tradition continued along its own lines, regardless of innovations introduced by the more sophisticated builders of the south and east.

The Long Houses of the Seventeenth Century

In these masonry districts, the walling of the domestic building had settled down to a standardized form of Elizabethan masonry, perfectly finished in the best tradition of the craft. The spans of stone lintels being limited, the windows remained stone-mullioned; the wide-span openings which the brick-builders covered with flat brick arches could not be provided until flat Renaissance arches constructed of wedge-shaped stone 'voussoirs' had been introduced from the Continent. Thus it was a long time before the seventeenth-century masons dared omit the central mullion of a cruciform window in order to provide an opening which could be filled with a sash window of Georgian type.

Thus during the seventeenth century we find the architectural belt which we know so well as the 'Cotswold' continuing in the Elizabethan tradition regardless of innovations. There are the mullioned windows with their heavy lintels and square moulded 'labels' round these. There are gablets finished with charming finials which are mediaeval pinnacles modified balusterwise to make some concession to Renaissance susceptibilities. There are mediaeval porches, sometimes showing Tudor arches, but occasionally having simple semicircular arches again making some concession to the new style of architectural ornament.

By the last quarter of the century the projecting labels had at last disappeared from the scene. Mullion construction, however, continued in use in smaller buildings until well into the next century, the masons being unwilling to span window lintels over more than eighteen inches or so.

The characteristic feature of the seventeenth-century farmhouse was the asymmetry of its long elevation due to the fact that the parlour on one side of its central stack was smaller than the principal room. This made it impossible to set out the principal elevation as a symmetrical 'show-front' in proper Renaissance manner. By the middle of the century, however, the Cotswold masons were deliberately making both rooms the same size. The fronts they created were wholly charming; the great chimney being flanked by a pair of three-storied gables forming a perfect composition with the projecting porch providing a key feature. These lovely frontispieces, at once the culmination and swan-song of English mediaeval domestic

108

19. A whitewashed cottage built by a Regency squire to re-house one of the families he had ejected from the old township of Milton Abbas in Dorset.

20. A dignified villa of Regency date at Box Hill in Surrey, its austerity lightened by its playful trellis porch.

architecture, had all too soon to abandon their soaring gables and welcoming porches to the 'foul torrent' of the Renaissance.

The Cotswold style continues its magnificent architectural tradition independently of the general trend of building technique. Adhering to the use of freestone—of which the region had a plentiful supply—it gradually abandoned its mediaeval features, such as the pinnacled gablet, and replaced its long mullioned windows with the cruciform window of Renaissance proportions. Still half a century or more behind the brick-building regions, the Cotswold builders at last took up the sash window, but set it in an opening now properly provided with a stone architrave in the best Renaissance manner.

Once the details of the Orders and their mouldings had been mastered, the masons of the freestone belt, from Northampton to Bath, were able to turn out small houses of an architectural perfection equal to anything the Continent could show, and far more distinguished than the products of the brick-building regions.

A large proportion of seventeenth-century long houses remaining today have been enlarged since their foundation to provide more liberal accommodation. During the century itself, parlourless houses frequently had the end stack doubled and a parlour built on beyond, while a single-parlour house might be provided with a dining-parlour at the lower end with a gable-stack for heating it.

Wings to long houses were appearing by about the time of the Restoration. The simplest form was the short projection containing a new parlour with chamber over; often a new and more impressive 'upper end' was created by this device (Fig. 10a). Or the additional accommodation might be doubled to form a complete wing with its own central stack and perhaps a new entrance with a 'show front' facing towards the interior of the 'L' (Fig. 10b). Or a wing might be added athwart the upper end of the original house to form a 'T' (Fig. 10c), either with a central stack or, later, displaying the pair of gable-stacks of the eighteenth century.

During the late-eighteenth and nineteenth centuries, after the 'long' house had become replaced by the 'square' type, houses were sometimes 'squared-up' by building the new accommodation alongside the original. This could be done either by rebuilding a rear outshot to full height (Fig. 15b), or by adding a new front block, with an impressive elevation. entirely concealing the original structure from view (Fig. 15a).

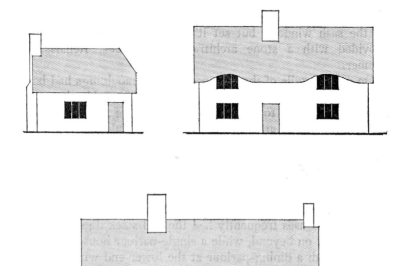

Long Houses

CHAPTER V

The Georgians

———— ❀ ————

By the end of the seventeenth century all traces of mediaevalism had disappeared from English architecture. The country was well supplied with architects, most of them with some experience of the Renaissance style of the Age. There were now plenty of examples of new buildings for the local builder/architects to copy, and several textbooks on architecture and building construction were available.

The single-span was disappearing except in the smallest houses. The squared-up house plan was now understood and simple 'squared paper' elevations with their rectangular openings symmetrically arranged could be designed by anyone with a moderate amount of intelligence. Modern construction was now understood by all. The country could produce plenty of bricks for use in stoneless areas and the timber frame had become obsolete. Chimney and fireplace construction was now standardized. While very humble houses still kept to the solid wood window-frame and the wrought-iron casement—more suitable to the horizontal (mediaeval) type of window still used in small buildings—most middle-class houses used the tall Renaissance window with its boxed sashes. Doorways were rectangular openings provided with some simple Renaissance motif for embellishment.

Other than the special treatment accorded the entrance doorway, there was little that was notable architecturally about the elevations of middle-class houses of the eighteenth century. At a time when the fashionable architects of the age were raising vast palaces, the brick houses of the style which was to become 'Georgian' relied for effect on compactness, proportions, and, above all, an orderly fenestration scheme.

111

The Georgians

Even in mediaeval times, the entrance front of the house had always been treated with some architectural consideration, as a 'show front'. But special treatment had been confined to isolated features of which, of course, the entrance doorway and its porch had been the most important. After this, the designers of larger houses had emphasized the great window lighting the dais, while in the farmhouse particular attention had been given to the first-floor window lighting the principal chamber—the 'chamber of estate'. But with the coming of the Renaissance no one window had been permitted precedence; each had to play its part as a unit of a fenestration system.

At the very beginning of the century, a slight echo of the greater monumentalism of mansion architecture may be seen in an occasional overlay of large arches superimposed on the house-front to form a series of tall arched recesses emphasizing the elevational scheme. But this rather pompous treatment was soon abandoned as unnecessary and costly.

The squared-up plans of the eighteenth-century houses were compact, with a ground floor of parlours and a kitchen; above were chambers and above these attics. The greater use of lead —and, later, slate—for low-pitched roofs enabled the old attic space to be improved to form a complete storey having proper window walls instead of dormers; this provided a fine three-storey elevation to the building and with a parapet concealing the roof gave a reasonable imitation of a contemporary Renaissance villa. At this time many existing houses were given a new front, sometimes of brickwork applied to reface an existing timber frame; such a face-lifting operation gave the owner a chance to improve the attic storey at the same time by including it in the new fenestration scheme.

The fundamental factor of Renaissance designs was symmetry about the main entrance to the building. During the previous century this had been asymmetrically placed between a large kitchen-living-room and a smaller parlour. Moreover it opened into a small porch at the back of which was the great chimney-stack. This very un-monumental arrangement could not be associated with Renaissance practice—the whole of the centre of the house would have to be redesigned.

One can sometimes find early-eighteenth century farm-houses where the designer of an old-fashioned 'long' house,

112

still clinging to its central chimney-stack, has set this in the exact centre of the building so as to provide the building with a symmetrical elevation. To do this, of course, he has had to reduce the kitchen to the same size as the parlour, doubtless a serious loss of working space to the farmer's wife.

At its inception, one of the reasons for the popularity of the central stack had been the service it rendered in providing a 'well' in which to accommodate the stair to the upper floor. This could, however, be moved outside the house and set in a projecting tower—a well-known Elizabethan feature in larger houses—or even worked in under the sloping roof of the 'outshot' (Fig. 13b). This last device was actually employed late in the seventeenth century for freeing the middle of the house from the obstructive stack, which was split up into separate ones for kitchen and parlour.

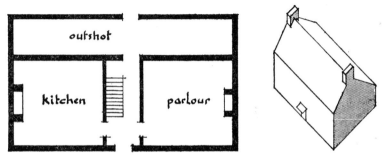

Fig. 14. *Georgian cottage*

The removal of the support provided by the great stack necessitated its replacement by a sturdily-framed partition for carrying the spinal floor beams or summers. That spanning the longer, kitchen, half of the plan was sometimes turned to pass athwart the building; an interesting variation which in a badly-mutilated old house will sometimes provide the clue as to which part was the original kitchen end.

The Georgian plan was to abolish for ever the great chimney stack and replace it with a pair of gable stacks in a small house (Fig. 14) or two pairs in the case of a squarish double-span plan (Fig. 12). The entrance could then be sited in the centre of the main front with access behind it to the parlours on either side. It was in this central area that the principal feature of the

113   H

Georgian house was situated—its staircase. In larger houses this remained on the square 'open well' plan of Elizabethan times. In lesser houses the 'pair of stairs' or dog-leg was employed. As the eighteenth century developed, the balusters became more slender and increased in number; the whole balustrade was lightened to become far more graceful than the stair of Restoration days.

The long mediaeval type of house plan glorified in its very attenuation—symbol of segregation between an upper and a lower end. But the square Georgian house needed a heart. This could be provided by its staircase, at once the most elegant architectural feature of the interior and the focus of all circulation between its rooms and storeys. Often it is so buried in the midst of the building that it can only be lit from above; hence the charming little cupola-capped turret light which is so often seen perched on the roof of the Georgian house. (Fig. 12).

The building revolution of the sixteenth century had followed the Dissolution of the Monasteries, that of the following century the Civil War. The most important factor in the development of Georgian building was the importation of softwood from Scandinavia. Now that the wood-framed building had become obsolete, there was no longer any need for timber of great strength. The improved method of laying floor joists provided floors which would carry any load required. What was wanted now was timber for joinery—doors, windows, staircases, carved ornament. The new timber could be far more easily worked than oak; Classical cornices, even, could be run far more easily than the hand-carved mouldings of Tudor days.

The difficulty was that this very softness gave the completed features less chance of surviving the assaults of the English climate. Softwood would not patinate to chisel-blunting hardness as the old oak did. Some means had to be found of protecting the timber from damp and decay.

The scientists of the period discovered that lead oxide, applied by solution in an oleaginous vehicle, would form a protective skin on the surface of the wood. Thus was discovered the value of 'paint' as a protective coat to wood. The substance was however called at this time 'lead oxide' and factories for its manufacture were opened along the Thames estuary. The colour of the painted timber became white; thus white paint is perhaps the most striking feature associated with Georgian architecture. Later on, the paint was tinted with some substance to restore the colour of the wood; coats of brown paint may sometimes be found remaining on eighteenth-century woodwork. But the tinting of paint in many colours and applied to large areas of joinery for decorative purposes is an invention of the nineteenth century.

In every age we find the owners of houses trying either to build themselves 'contemporary' homes or else to 'modernize' their existing ones. The concern of the Georgian house-owner was what to do with his antiquated timber-framed building. Some form of 'cladding' was needed to conceal the old timberwork and if possible include within its treatment some new windows of fashionable proportion and finish.

It had been the custom of builders working along the southeastern coasts of England to sheathe their house-frames externally in boarding covered with pitch and caulked as in shipbuilding; this served to prevent driving rain and spray from penetrating between frame and filling.

The same idea was adopted by other house-builders in the region and its littoral, who used softwood boards called 'weatherboards' or 'clapboards' and fixed them, overlapping as in ship construction, to cover the house frames. The whole sheathing was, of course, painted white with 'lead oxide'.

The obvious development from covering old timber houseframes with clapboarding was to build new houses with *softwood* frames and sheath them with boarding. Towards the end of the century, and during the Regency, large numbers of buildings of this sort appeared in the south and east of England. Not only were impecunious house builders and providers of cottages for farm staff using this method of construction, but the new industrial buildings of the age—mills, workshops, and the like—were being erected as cheaply as possible in framed construction with a covering of boards. The white water-mills of southern England remain today as examples of a charming architectural style.

In the eastern States of North America, the system of construction was developed to a monumental degree, as witness the lovely 'Colonial' mansions of that countryside.

The softwood framing was set out rather differently than the older hardwood frames, with the 'studs' nearer together to carry the external boarding and the inner skin of lath and plaster. There was no infilling or 'nogging' and the 'studding' was strengthened by raking 'braces' at the angles and elsewhere—the same system exists to this day for the construction of internal partitions.

But brick was still the principal material for house-building, and beautiful clean-cut red bricks were produced and laid with

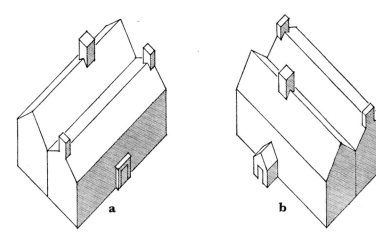

Fig. 15. Squaring-up the long house of the seventeenth century—
late-eighteenth and nineteenth centuries
(a) by building new block across front of old house
(b) by rebuilding a rear outshot to full height

their bonding forming a perfect pattern of fine joints on a rich red wall. The craftsmen of the brickmaking regions were taking as much pride in their walling as had their forebears the mediaeval freemasons. During the seventeenth century there is clear evidence of older traditions; stone quoins might be used, or stone dressings round openings. Even in the Georgian period one finds the bricklayers imitating the projecting 'rusticated' quoins of the stonemasons in tortured brick. But by the middle of the eighteenth century the bricklayers have become entirely confident in their medium and its potentialities. One of the most delightful Georgian devices is the use of over-burnt black 'headers' or *grizels* to form a diaper pattern over the wall-face.

With the development of brickmaking the craft of tile-making developed also. In the clay regions, many a thatched roof was stripped and recovered in tile. The Sussex hips, however—relics of the old thatches—were allowed to remain and achieved a new charm in red-brown tile, today often glorified with golden lichen.

The art of shingling is as old as English building. The house-frames of the days of the Norman Conquest were sheathed with shingles, as were the roofs of many a great cathedral centuries later. During the eighteenth century, the same principle was revived using clay tiles instead of shingles, so that many a house-frame—especially in the case of an upper storey left exposed after the ground floor had been rebuilt in brickwork—was sheathed in the same tiling used to replace the roof-thatch (13).

But there can be no doubt that wherever possible the house-owner of the late-eighteenth century tried to provide himself with a *white* house. The great mansion was either stone or plastered with stucco (everyone has heard of King George's horrified exclamation when being shown his Prime Minister's new home—'*brick*, Mr. Pitt, *brick*!'). More and more people were having houses built for them, most of them of course in brick. It was necessary to try to rise above brick if possible—or at least to rise above its plebeian colour. So many a brick house was just covered with stucco, and many an old house-frame was simply sheathed in lath and plaster.

Plaster had been used externally, as early as the Jacobean era, for covering over the rough 'nogging' filling the panelled house-frames of that period; the craftsmen being mostly from the Low Countries, the eastern side of England has benefited most from their art—for some of the ornament lavished on the magnificent ceilings of the age strayed out to the 'pargetted' panels of the house-front.

During the Regency, gleaming white was the proper colour for a gentleman's house; even the brick walling of humbler homes was whenever possible concealed behind a mask of stucco (19).

117

The Georgians

Augustus of Rome was for building renowned
For of marble he left, what of brick he had found.
But is not our NASH, too, a very great master—
He finds us all brick . . .

and leaves us all plaster!

Where bricks, flint, or field stone were readily available, the latter part of the eighteenth century often saw the whole of the main elevation of a house completely refaced with a new front wall which effectively concealed the rustic origins of the building behind it.

Sometimes such alterations were more comprehensive. Many of the humbler houses of the seventeenth century had their chamber floors entirely contained within the roof-space and lighted only by small windows in the end gables and perhaps a couple of small gablets contrived on the front of the building and absorbed beneath the undulations of the thatch. Nowadays one can often clearly detect, by noting a change of materials in the upper part of a gable end, where the roof of such a humble home has been raised during the eighteenth century to provide better headroom for the chamber floor.

All such restorations of an old house usually included if possible an attempt to make at least the main front of the building appear symmetrical. Often a great central stack prevented this being done, but at least the new elevation could be tidied up and its windows set out in regular form and provided with boxed sashes to fit the fashion.

The tall sash window is the essential feature of every Georgian house. At the beginning of the century its glazing bars had been very thick and its panes only slightly taller than the square. By the middle of the century the bars had become more slender and the panes had settled down to approximately one and a quarter widths high (actually the diagonal on the width squared often provides the height). Both sashes were sliding up and down instead of one only.

The stone 'dressings' of the mediaeval window had, of course, formed part of the wall-face. When wooden window-frames had been introduced these had been set back only very slightly in their 'reveals' so that while receiving some slight protection from the weather they still appeared flush-set as were stone-set windows. But when the wide box-frames were introduced into London it was found that fire could spread from room to room, building to building, by leaping across between window frames. In 1709, therefore, orders were given that in future they were to be set back at least four inches from the wall-face. This ordinance, soon to be followed by another ordering the boxes to be tucked away behind the outer brick-work, set an architectural fashion which spread into the rural areas and nowadays provides a useful aid in dating early eighteenth-century houses.

A later development in fenestration was a reappearance of the bay window which had passed from the scene with the great halls of the Elizabethans. Georgian bays were, however, seldom more than one storey in height except in the case of tall town houses. The new technique of joist-laying enabled joists to be 'jettied out' to a distance of several feet and made to carry an oriel window of similar form to the contemporary bay —another reappearance of a fine feature of mediaeval domestic architecture.

Towards the end of the century the 'Venetian' or 'Palladian' window, with its rounded central portion and narrow square-headed side lights, becomes popular as an axial feature. In smaller houses the central wide light is generally the same height as the side ones and has no arched head to it; at the beginning of the nineteenth century the whole of the house fenestration might consist of these charming 'triptych' windows.

A complete innovation which we owe to the later Georgian builders is the bow window with its sweeping arc projecting only slightly from the building face. The pattern of glazing bars containing the glass always makes these bows attractive, never more so than when they are employed as shop fronts framing the display of goods on the stall-board behind. A feature of the Renaissance shop-front was the transference of the external mediaeval stall-board to the inside of the window.

With bays, oriels, bows and Venetian windows there were plenty of opportunities for the Georgian builders to vary the fenestration of their elevations and concentrate attention on any particular portion, particularly the centre line. The 'aedicule' —the complete Renaissance frame with architrave, entablature, and perhaps a pediment—was only used in the finest houses and does not appear in lesser domestic architecture.

The Classical pediment, however, is often used, from the very beginning of the eighteenth century, not as a crowning feature to a Palladian portico, but as an upward swelling of the parapet in the centre of an elevation, especially over the main entrance.

The parapet with box gutter behind it is employed in Georgian buildings as in those of mediaeval days. Renaissance taste, however, always called for a cornice to finish a wall-top, thus a parapet is generally set as a 'blocking-course' above a cornice.

The roofs of Georgian buildings vary considerably, even those newly constructed being of various forms. With the adoption of the squared-up plan, and the development of the 'four-elevation' design, the obvious thing to do was to finish each of these with a classical cornice in stone, stuccoed brick, or woodwork. This means that the roof had to be 'hipped' all round, rising as it were from the cornice. Thus the gable disappears more and more from the Georgian scene and tall chimney-stacks rise from the edges of the building, unsupported by gables, and appearing far more like the old wall stacks of mediaeval days. (Fig. 12).

A feature of late-eighteenth century small houses is the use of the double-pitch roof which gives better headroom in an attic storey. This type of roof was introduced into France by the architect Mansard and is called to this day a 'mansard' roof (24).

Although the Georgian planners had returned to the mediaeval practice of building chimney-stacks in external walls they did so with the big distinction that the stack projected *inside* the building so as not to break up the smooth run of the exterior elevation. In doing this they created obstructions inside their rooms and found themselves faced with awkward alcoves on either side of the chimney breast. With Renaissance skill they designed charming niches for the display of contemporary china. Usually round-headed, these Georgian niches were often ceiled with semi-domes or charmingly-devised shell forms moulded in plaster. From internal niches the shells were brought outside to grace the hoods over entrance doorways.

The chimney-stack had lost most of its glamour by Georgian

days, having been reduced to a simple rectangular affair with no ornamentation other than a cornice. From the beginning of the century there were panels on the sides of the stack but even these were abandoned as too expensive. The chimney-stack rising above eaves is a weak construction and it is not uncommon to see these tall shafts leaning over, either through the sinking of some chimney beam below or through unequal settlement of the joints of the brickwork due to prevailing winds or the heat of the summer sun.

The commonest type of village residence to be met with today is still the seventeenth-century farmhouse with its central stack dividing the long ridge into two parts for kitchen and parlour. On the other hand, the big stack with its double fireplace took up a strip of the house some six to eight feet wide; we often find, therefore, that it has been taken out during the eighteenth century or later and the space given over to a staircase or otherwise replanned into the accommodation. But the asymmetry of the long house-front remains as a clear indication of the early date of the house, even though a Georgian pair of end stacks may have been added, like a pair of ears, at the gable ends to take the place of the vanished central feature. (Fig. 16b).

The Georgian house showed itself in a diversity of forms. In addition to dwelling houses proper there were subsidiary buildings such as the lodge in which the gate-keeper of a mansion lived; there was also the public lodge—the toll-house where the keeper lived who opened the turnpike gates to travellers and took the toll paid for passage. There were also groups of almshouses—some of them large clusters fringing a courtyard and others just two or four little lodgings in a row— built by rich landowners to house the indigent poor of the parish. Some of these were architecturally fine, while others were of quite humble character without benefit of sash window.

During the latter part of the eighteenth century a number of trades were being practised in the village homes. Tailor, baker, wheelwright are but samples of a score or so of tradesmen who used a ground-floor parlour as a workshop. Their one-time occupation of such a room is often evidenced by the improvement of its fenestration; thus the eighteenth-century workshop window is usually five lights wide instead of the normal domestic three.

121

It was the upper middle-class houses which made the best show with their fine elevations and hipped roofs. Rural farmhouses still followed quite a humble ordinance. They were often single-span to facilitate the provision of a spacious farm-kitchen, in which case their accommodation would probably be augmented by wide 'outshots'. They displayed Georgian façades along their main fronts but the simple 'fascia' which carried the rainwater gutter at the eaves was echoed by 'barge boards' projecting from the gable-ends.

The glory of a Georgian house-front was its main doorway. It might be surrounded by a Renaissance 'architrave mould', crowned perhaps by a complete Classic entablature of frieze and cornice. It might be flanked by pilasters or columns, the latter perhaps free-standing and carrying a small porch roof. At the close of the seventeenth century a popular feature of the urban doorway had been a door-hood carried on elaborately-carved brackets; this feature—one of the first Renaissance innovations to be encountered by the English builders—was by them never forgotten. Almost to the present day the village builders have been devising every conceivable variation of the bracketed door-hood—perhaps the most charming and ubiquitous sign-manual of the English vernacular.

This is not the book in which to describe the countless enchanting architectural details of what is undoubtedly our best loved domestic building style—that essentially English vernacular presentation of the European Renaissance which we call the Georgian and which displays in particular such an amazing variety of devices for the embellishment of the entrance doorway. Once the style had become established in this country, copying by one carpenter or mason from another was clearly eschewed; each vied rather in the ingenuity with which to ring the changes on a few simple elements to produce an infinite variety of treatments, to our never-ending delight.

To study English Rural Renaissance architecture at its best, examine the doorways which line the village streets of England. Every conceivable motif ever invented by the great men of Renaissance architecture may be seen reproduced in humble fashion by those faithful architects, the builders of rural England. Every shape of hood, every contour of bracket, you may see it there. As new materials come into use, they are brought into the picture. Zinc and even the now-despised corrugated iron, the cast-iron panels of the beginning of the nineteenth century, the trellis-work (20) and rustic timbers of the Romantic period.

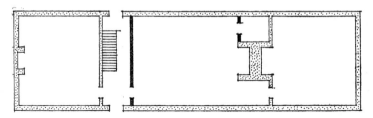

(*a*) *provision of new stair replacing original spiral*

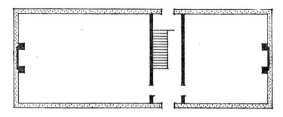

(*b*) *the same but involving removal of the central stack and its replacement by one at each gable end*

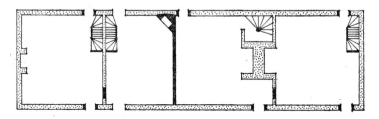

(*c*) *conversion to a row of four cottages*

Fig. 16. Georgian modifications to the plans of seventeenth century long houses

Everything is reflected in the little cottage door-hoods and porches of village England.

If it comes to 'keeping up with the neighbours' there is no

more rewarding device than augmenting the dignity of one's front door. If we review the general building situation in this country at the beginning of the eighteenth century, we find that the spread of well-built houses from south and east to north and west is continuing. Intermixed with brickwork, the well-constructed timber frames of the latter part of the seventeenth century have covered the north-west Midlands as far as the Welsh Marches. The stone belt is filled with fine houses while the neighbouring chalk areas are using flint to good effect.

It is now the turn of the rubble-stone builders of West and North to provide houses for their regions. The long seventeenth-century plan with the central stack is followed (Fig. 9); stairs are either caracoles or steep enclosed stairs partly straight and part winding. Windows are of mullioned type constructed in wood; roofs either framed or incorporating heavy trusses of king- or queen-post type, covered with tile-stone or slate.

The roof of the Georgian house depends for its stability upon its heavy trusses or 'principals'. During the latter part of the seventeenth century, roof construction had deteriorated owing to the abandoning of proper trusses in favour of a less-obstructive form of roof framed up like a floor and having the same weak joints where timbers met. The Georgians returned to the proper Renaissance king-post truss and also employed a variation of the queen-post truss in which the posts were replaced by curved struts directly supporting the purlins.

In the clothing districts of Yorkshire, the mid-seventeenth century produced houses of the multi-gabled Cotswold type but built of rubble stone and lacking the refinements of the more southerly style which, of course, owed so much of its quality to the excellence of its freestone. It was really the eighteenth century which saw the rapid development of stone building in Yorkshire; at its close the industrialized regions in particular were being well provided with multi-storey Georgian-type houses in rubble stone, this being followed during the next century by dressed stonework of a quality which may be equal to that of the Bath region.

In the West, cob is often substituted for rubble stone, and thatch for stone tile or slate. A charming feature of much of the northern and western building is the use of limewash on rubble stone elevations (11).

Thus during the eighteenth century, most villages were provided with well-built houses for farmers and smallholders, so that rural England in the Georgian era was in process of creating the pattern of village streets so familiar to us today. During the eighteenth century there were many more classes of domestic buildings than heretofore. At the top of the tree were the mansions of the nobility. Below this came a stratum of country squires whose fine country houses often boasted a pillared 'Palladian' portico. Still lower were the houses of the lesser squirearchy, the parsonages, and the homes of the better-endowed professional men; perhaps together with these were the larger farmhouses with the semi-mediaeval domestic organization of their farm staff.

In the towns we have the growth of the 'terrace' of houses, each on its narrow frontage, with the beginnings of monumental town-planning appearing in 'squares', 'crescents', 'circuses' and 'paragons' (polygons).

But now an entirely new type of house is appearing—the labourer's cottage. What we call a cottage today is probably the house built for a man who in his day was a person of property. The contemporary peasant or farm labourer would have lived in a hovel built with his own hands and owing nothing to architecture or building science.

But the Georgian Age was an age of great agricultural prosperity, and bred a race of country squires who were immensely proud of their landed property. Not only did they rival each other in the excellence of their crops and herds; their holdings were models of well-planned, well-kept estates indicating their owners' determination to lose no chance of surrounding themselves with every aspect of rural charm.

They embellished their homes with parterres, perrons, walled gardens, gazebos, lawns, shrubberies, and every sort of floral entertainment. They planted trees in great numbers—as avenues leading to their porticoes, along the hedgerows to give shade to cattle, and in the park-land pastures immediately adjoining their mansions.

They built coach-houses and stabling round well-paved courtyards.

They also built homes for their farm staff. In this at last we have the true cottage, built by a builder, at the squire's command, for a labourer on his estate.

The cottage of late-Georgian and later times can be recognized immediately by its small rooms, very poky when compared with the wide single-span apartments of the seventeenth-century farmhouses. (But the conversion of so many of these farmhouses during 'Enclosure' days often included the subdivision of the spacious old rooms by internal partitions so as to provide rooms of 'cottage' dimensions.)

The earliest true cottages were usually just a simple kitchen-living-room with a bedchamber over. At this time was invented the 'semi-detached' plan with two such cottages set on either side of a central chimney-stack. Sometimes there is an 'outshot' at the rear for a wash-house; there may even be a double-span plan to provide a parlour as well as a kitchen. It was through these cottages, sometimes arranged along a lane or around a green, that the country squires demonstrated to each other their humanity and liberality of thought, as well as their skill in augmenting the actual value of their estates.

The England we see today, in so far as the countryside is concerned, is really Georgian England. The villages of ancient houses—'cottages' you will call them—have for the most part been Georgianized even though their windows may still be long and low and mullioned in mediaeval fashion.

During the course of the Georgian Age the face of England became transformed through the industry of the 'Turnpike Trusts'. By the end of the seventeenth century the main routes between towns had been secured and all-weather river-crossings established. Now it was the turn of the country villages to be joined one to another and cross-country routes for supplying them with goods in exchange for their produce set out and maintained by a system of tolls collected at the hundreds of toll houses with which they were lined. These through routes provided new sites for building labourers' cottages. More particularly they became the focus for façades of country houses newly founded on roadside sites as well as causing the frontispieces of existing houses to be reorientated towards them. Thus in this age of enclosure the wastes and commons were pierced and opened out by the new road systems and sown with wayside hamlets with here and there a new farmhouse or country residence.

The Georgian road may have been macadamized but it is still the road of the stage-coach and the highwayman; the hollyhocks in the cottage gardens are the same as those he saw as he rode by. The squire's house—whatever may be its present status—still peeps at us through the tree-filled park. The hedgerows and the avenues are those he planted when he

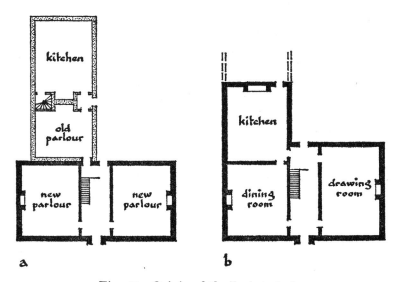

Fig. 17. *Origin of the L-shaped plan*
(*a*) *late-eighteenth century enlargement of earlier 'long' house*
(*b*) *nineteenth century house with kitchen sited in wing at rear of main block*

made his drive and set out his fields and meadows on the site of the great grim common fields of mediaeval days. The tall elm and the white sash-window—both are Georgian.

The building style which we know as Georgian is that which developed during the eighteenth century and is for the most part founded upon red brick walling with simple openings and white-painted windows and cornices (23). It was a product of the brick-building regions of the south and east of England. The stone-building belt, and the North of England, were slow to change their ways. A four-centred arch may often be encountered here, over doorway or fireplace, long after such mediaeval anachronisms had disappeared from more sophisticated districts. The stonemasons were studying the new fashion, but were still rather slow at following it.

When, however, towards the end of the century, the stone-building belt from Somerset to Northampton at last took up the style, it produced very fine Renaissance houses complete with every refinement properly turned out in faultless masonry. The Bath region is particularly notable for its series of lovely stone houses—pure High Renaissance in character rather than of that warm lively red-brick style which is the true Georgian of England.

There can be no doubt that the Renaissance building style, in its Georgian form, captivated English taste. Not only were there new houses building, but wherever the site permitted we can often find where a complete new Georgian wing with a fine entrance front has been added at right-angles to an earlier building the old low rooms of which remain at the rear as kitchen and stores. (Fig. 17). The 'L'-shaped house, thus fortuitously arrived at, was copied by the nineteenth-century builders as a device for relegating the kitchen with its offices to a subsidiary wing projecting from the rear of the main building. The 'ell', however, never played in this country the important part it did in North American domestic architecture.

By the turn of the century, even the humble cottage built by the English squire for his farm labourer was a Georgian house in miniature; its central doorway with stair hall behind separating the two tiny parlours each with its small chimney-stack. (Fig. 14). These charming little 'dolls' houses', so simple in design, mock us today with fingers of scorn pointing at our lop-sided 'universal plan' houses and our monstrously over-roofed 'bungalows'.

The interiors of Georgian houses show considerable change from the manners of the previous century. The fireplace is the same rectangular opening, but its surrounding frame is often a bulging 'bolection' moulding—a distant echo of the Continental Baroque. Towards the end of the century the new iron foundries of the Midlands were beginning to turn out cast-iron 'interiors' which fitted into the fireplace and took care of the coal now

128

21. An early-nineteenth century rustic villa at Winterbourne Came in Dorset which illustrates the Romantic Reaction to the Industrial Revolution. The factory-made iron glazing bars of the windows are worked into a fanciful pattern.

22. A nineteenth-century 'Romantic' cottage in the New Forest which displays in its fenestration its sympathy towards the Gothic Revival.

becoming a popular fuel. These early grates are tall constructions having a hob on either side with the grate itself suspended high above the hearth; the grate-front is a series of heavy bars framed in a drooping semicircle while this is supported by another semicircular arch rising from the hearth itself. (During the 'Regency Gothic' period at the turn of the century, the ironmasters were turning out the same type of 'birds-nest' grate but having ornament in 'Gothick' style instead of Renaissance.)

Another sign of the approach of the industrial age is shown in the cast-iron windows which appeared at this time. They were complete with frames and glazing bars—sometimes even with Gothic arched heads—and were provided with 'hooks and bands', cockspur fasteners, and stays for holding open these forerunners of the steel windows of today.

The iron 'interior' spelt the end of the open fire on the hearth with its back and dogs. The new fuel was now being properly contained and stoking was a much less energetic affair causing far less damage to the jambs of the fireplace opening. Thus wooden surrounds to this opening could be developed without fear from injury during stoking operations.

Even at the end of the Georgian period there were still many who could not afford to pay joiners to construct the elaborate box-frames which housed the Georgian sashes. Nor, in some cases, were their rooms high enough to take tall sash-windows. So in lesser homes the low, long, mullioned mediaeval type of window continued in use throughout the Georgian era, coming into its own again with the Romantic age of the Regency Gothic.

A new apartment was appearing in the English house of the eighteenth century. The Great Hall of mediaeval days had vanished, even in the largest mansions, during the seventeenth century, being replaced by an entrance hall entered from the main doorway, providing direct access to the principal ground floor parlours, and having at its rear the grand staircase. These huge apartments, called *salons* in France, were for purposes of entertainment, not for general use but for special occasions only. The *salon* of a great house gave its name to the assembly held in it—a gathering of wealth and beauty comparable to the Royal Courts.

The town house could not have a true *salon*; its plan was too restricted. Unlike the country houses, the principal apartments of the town house were, in Renaissance fashion, on the *piano nobile*—the first floor. One of the first floor parlours was designated the 'withdrawing room', and this apartment was developed—often by letting it run from front to back of the house —as an urban counterpart of the nobleman's *salon*. The 'drawing-room' thus became a part of the urban residence—giving its name to the seasonal assemblies held in it—and thence spread throughout English domestic architecture became the designation of the most important of the parlours.

One of the disadvantages of the Renaissance plan with its centralized entrance dividing the front of the building into two was that this debarred the architects from setting out a large apartment—in the style of the Great Hall of mediaeval days —along the main elevation. But the abandoning, during the eighteenth century, of the obstructive internal chimney-stack enabled a pair of front and back parlours to be joined together to form a long room passing from front to back of the house. This is very often the form taken by the drawing-room of the Georgian country house. (Fig. 12).

The living-room floor set directly upon the surface of the ground provides very cold accommodation; thus during the seventeenth century the cellar becomes popular as insulation. The semi-basements of the contemporary town house provided space for the kitchen and its offices; the same device introduced into the country house enabled the Georgians to raise the ground floor into a *piano nobile* reached by a fine flight of steps.

Since the days of the great halls, entered through carved screenwork and terminated by a dais lit through magnificent glass, no one seemed to have paid much attention to the provision of any monumental treatment—other than applied ornament—to the principal apartment of a private house. Until the Renaissance era, little attention had been given to the proportions of ordinary rooms. But the habit of gracious living had become part of the soul of Regency England. The Georgians, in their spacious way, expanded the earlier bay window into a wide trilateral embracing the whole width of the room and providing its occupants with a panoramic view of park or garden. In Regency days, the softer lines of the swelling bow window found an echo in the gracefully bowed end which could be employed to lend charm and dignity to the Regency drawing-room.

The most striking difference to be found in the interior of the Georgian house would have been its furniture. The seventeenth-century house, though in itself a product of the Renaissance, was still furnished in what was little advanced beyond mediaeval fashion. There was the refectory table still to the fore (with a promise of things to come in the well-joinered gate-leg). There were benches and stools, with here and there an uncomfortable high-back chair.

But the eighteenth century saw the development of furniture in England, with its great names which are still household words today. And this filling of the interiors of houses with furniture had an interesting effect on interior decoration.

For plastered walls soon began to suffer badly from the backs of chairs pushed against them. The result was the introduction of the 'chair-rail' or 'dado-rail' at a height of some three feet from the wall to protect its plaster. And the invention of the chair-rail introduced a new feature into the house—the dado.

This innovation completely changed the ordinance of wall panelling. The old grillage of earlier days gave place to a system of much larger panels, tall ones above the chair-rail and low ones in the dado. The widths of the panels had to be increased to suit the new module. The large panels presented some difficulties to the joiners, who invented a new system of paring down or bevelling their edges so as to fit them into grooves cut into the framing. These 'fielded' panels are products of the Georgian era; sometimes a feature is made of the change from the flat to the bevelled surfaces.

Internal doors, and to some extent the external ones also, had to change their character to meet the new system of panelling. The doors were now given a wide 'lock rail' at the same level as the chair-rail; the same ordinance of tall panels above short ones was followed in the doors and has remained so until recent years when the advent of the sheathed 'flush' door has introduced yet another innovation into interior design.

The use of strong frames for hanging internal doors was given up after about the middle of the century in all except humble houses. The panelling was taken round into the door opening as a 'lining' and the door hung to it. An opening 'lined' in this fashion could be used with or without an architrave. If the former, the feature could be developed into an 'overdoor' with an 'entablature' or even a small pediment.

With the advent of the Georgian type of internal panelling there appeared also the internal cornice to finish it off and ease the junction between wall and ceiling. First of joinery, the cornice eventually became formed in plaster, an innovation which has continued in use, through many modifications of its original Classical silhouette, almost to the present time.

The old casement window—by the end of the Georgian period revived as a wooden sash hinged instead of sliding—had been hung on the crude iron hooks which, forged by the local smith who made the nails, were also used for hanging doors to their frames. Even in mediaeval days the hinge with its pin had been known and large and elaborate examples of it had been made. The old strap hinge had been a complex affair having a vertical portion for fixing to the frame and a horizontal strap which passed right across the door and helped to tie all its timbers together.

With the advent of the framed door, the strap part of the hinge became obsolete and was redesigned as a small 'L' turning the corner of the door. The hinge was still fixed to the face of the frame and door—not to the adjoining edges as with the modern 'butt' hinge. The eighteenth-century hinge is often a charming piece of wrought-iron with its ends formed into 'seahorse' shapes displayed with good effect on both door and frame.

The Georgian era is the wrought-iron age. By the last quarter of the previous century most large mansions had been provided with systems of fence-walls of brick punctuated with piers, often with stone cornices finished with urns and other types of Renaissance finial. In order to open up the forecourts and other areas where some seclusion was desired without too much of a claustral effect, the fence walls were broken up into bays divided by piers and filled with wrought-iron railings (23).

The small houses of the Georgian era adopted this system of erecting lines of railings with great effect, and expanded the decorative scheme to include entrance gates which often show in their designs a very high degree of skill on the part of the

craftsman. The units used are comparatively few in number—
the S-curve, the C-curve, the spearhead, the leaf and the
tendril. Everything was hand-forged and each unit riveted to
its neighbours. Thus could the village smith join the other
craftsmen in adding to the beauty of the Georgian house.

It should be noted that the smiths never trespassed into the
sphere of the joiner by producing such features as 'consoles' for
supporting door-hoods. There were, however, a great many
objects such as lamp brackets and the various items of kitchen-
fireplace equipment, which the smiths not only produced, but
embellished with many pleasant little tricks of the craftsman in
wrought-iron. The inn-sign bracket is, of course, a highly
suitable object for such treatment and many of the eighteenth-
century wrought-iron sign brackets still adorn our country
pubs.

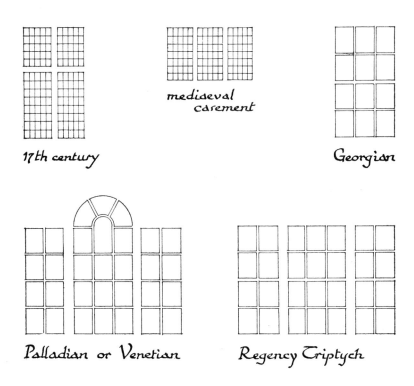

17th century   mediaeval casement   Georgian

Palladian or Venetian   Regency Triptych

CHAPTER VI

The Nineteenth Century

During the Elizabethan Age a certain cultural aura had become distinguishable, hovering over some of the nobility and obscuring much of the underlying mediaeval savagery. During the following century this faded before the onslaught of a new fanaticism culminating in the Civil War wherein all classes indulged themselves in primaeval savagery. Only the rustic poets, painters and musicians kept the stream of culture flowing.

By the Georgian Age the country had settled down to fulfil its destiny under the race of country gentlemen who had taken the place of the feudal lords and who vied with each other in demonstrating the beauty and richness of their estates. They had wealth and leisure, they were well-fed and energetic.

Not only England but the Continent as well was now opened up and made safe for travel. So travel became the hobby of the period. It had to be travel with an object, so it was travel in search of culture. No longer was the landowner an illiterate chieftain, he was a gentleman educated at a good school and at a university—to be taught, not how to earn a living, but the humanities. He could quote Latin and was familiar with the writers of Classical days—so the obvious thing to do was to travel to Rome. Thus from the hard-headed, hard-fisted, hard-riding Georgian squire develops the cultured Corinthian of the Regency who had been on the Grand Tour and met his elegant contemporaries in Paris and Florence.

An important factor in the society of the late-eighteenth century was the novel, the development of which, by encouraging reading for entertainment, not only raised the cultural level of the literate but broadened the element of imagination and even fantasy in literature. This was at a time when industrialism was firmly established in a number of centres; English iron-foundries for example were well in advance of the field. Industrialism, while stimulating the mental prowess of the nation, at the same time sponsored a reaction towards the pleasanter, idler, things in life. The Midland squire saw the fantastic shape of a great iron bridge rising across the local river; he turned towards the ruin of the mediaeval castle for reassurance and when he got home picked up, with a sigh, some romantic novel his wife had received from London.

A fashion for novels with a mediaeval setting produced a spontaneous effect upon architecture. As if suddenly conscious of their own national heritage, and ashamed of having slipped into the ways of foreigners, house-builders vied with each other in recreating 'Gothick' (for their Classical upbringing forced them to admit its barbaric origin) features of all descriptions. There were no masons to carry out the designs, so the builders had to resort to plaster, refining their detail to much slimmer proportions to suit the change in material.

Having no knowledge whatsoever of the origin and development of the features they used, they felt no restraint about exercising their skill to the full in creating beautiful designs of a richness and refinement to which none but a pedant could take exception. This devoted style of architecture, sometimes known as 'Regency Gothic', is also called 'Strawberry Hill Gothic' in recognition of the fact that Horace Walpole's house was one of its earliest and most notable examples. Its most monumental achievement was Fonthill Abbey, Beckford's vast creation of which only a humble fragment remains.

One of the delightful aspects of the architecture of the late-Georgian and Regency era is the enthusiasm with which all classes of craftsmen seized upon the current fashion and followed its feeling to the very best of their powers. While the big builders were able to provide turrets, masonry, battlements, beautifully joinered window tracery and fretted barge boards, their rural imitators provided the same ogival departures from the rigid Classic by making triangular heads to windows and lights in timber or brickwork. Any little 'Gothick' feature which could be simply constructed was attempted. Never has English taste so heartily approved of an architectural fashion as in those romantic days of Strawberry Hill.

One of the delights of the 'Gothick' revival was the re-introduction of the mediaeval gable and its ancient corollary, the barge board, the Regency house-builders making great play with this attractive feature. With leaded lights coming back into mullioned windows, as time went on, early nineteenth-century foundries produced iron casements having glazing bars patterned into groups of hexagonal panes (21) echoing the leaded 'quarries' of earlier days but offering better wind-resisting properties.

It will be appreciated that there were many who opposed this barbarous 'Gothick' style of building. True Classicists would have none of it; it was reactionary, retrograde. For these stern scholars the trumpet sounded when two English architects, Stuart and Revett, penetrated the bandit-ridden Balkans and reached Athens. The measured drawings which they brought home and published produced a revolution in the architecture of Europe and America. For here at last was the true Classical architecture; not the second-hand Hellenistic of Rome or the ill-digested Classicism of the Renaissance. The true Greek Orders—including the massive Doric which had never been seen before—burst upon England in stone and wood and plaster as a stern counter-attack aimed at the Romantics.

The conflict which followed is unique in the history of architecture. Two completely different styles were abroad in the land. The rivalry between Whig and Tory was as nothing compared with the Battle of the Styles. The professional architects—less dictatorial and more accommodating than today—swotted up both styles and dispensed either as required. A few of the leading architects of the day sportingly took up sides and kept the pot vigorously a-boiling.

During the second half of the nineteenth century this archi-tectural imbroglio became more than ever complicated as a result of the researches undertaken by numbers of unqualified individuals, limited in scope and heavily biased against Roman Catholics, Moslems, and Byzantine Greeks, into every aspect of architectural history. As a result of their activities, the Georgian style, having merged into the dainty Regency with every promise of unimaginable beauty ahead, reacted into the stern

Doric of Early Victorian days and then exploded into a welter of ill-digested 'Styles of Architecture' which even engulfed smaller houses such as parsonages. When, after the shock of the first Great War, English architectural style compromised by retreating into the melancholy Neo-Georgian of the nineteen-twenties, it may have been hoped that the past would be erased so that architecture as an art might begin again where it had left off. But in the meantime, steel and concrete had replaced to a great extent the traditional methods of building—the gap had become far too wide to bridge. Thus the principal contribution of the nineteenth century to the story of English architectural style had been, alas, one of mis-applied scholarship.

Towards the close of the eighteenth century, while rival forces were being marshalled for exciting new battles in the cause of Taste, a saddening chapter in the history of the old houses of the English countryside was being brought to a close. At the beginning of the century, rural England had still presented the sombre mediaeval spectacle of great bleak open fields of arable upon which individual holdings had been scattered piecemeal in unrelated strips. By its second quarter, however, the Georgian commissioners had begun a complete redistribution of these by gathering them together to form self-contained holdings which are the farms we know today. The squire seized on the occasion to surround himself with a pleasant tree-filled park, and as hedgerows began to grow along the boundaries of the new fields the English countryside began to unveil to us the lovely countenance it does today.

Well-endowed farmers abandoned their old homes in the township and built Georgian farmhouses on their new holdings, the subdividing of their old houses for the better accommodation of villagers producing the cottage rows of which most of our village architecture is composed (16) (17).

There was yet another reason for the abandoning of earlier farmhouses. For many farmers, the Enclosure Acts of Georgian days spelt disaster as the new preoccupation with the breeding of bloodstock prompted the introduction of legislation forcing farmers to fence their pastures to prevent their animals from straying, while an increased interest in agriculture brought about by the Napoleonic blockade brought still further pressure upon the farmers to enclose their land. Many of the smaller farmers were unable to afford the cost of the fencing required and were forced to sell out to adjoining landowners who might be affluent enough to provide the necessary enclosure. The merging of farms meant that many farmhouses became redundant. Their owners vacated them and went to work as farmhands for the new owners of the property. The old houses were, fortunately, not pulled down; they were, however, divided up into cottage rows for the accommodation of farm staff. It is in this guise that so many of them may be met with today, both in the depths of the countryside and lining the lanes of the villages. (Fig. 16c).

The long single-span houses of Elizabethan and seventeenth-century date were ideal for conversion. A two-parlour house could be made into three cottages by adding two new entrance doorways and two new staircases. The great central chimney-stack and the gable stack for the lower parlour were probably already in existence. Steep stairs were soon cut through the chamber floors. New doorways were easily made—it is interesting to note that many of the converting landowners were sufficiently concerned with the appearance of the front of the building to provide the new doors with some sort of architectural treatment, if only a bracketed door-hood.

So today these old farmhouses, in their disguise as 'rows of cottages', are still left to us, made possibly even more attractive by their cottage doorways embellished with every device known to the rustic carpenter. If we look up to the roofs, we may see here and there a great chimney of Jacobean or Elizabethan days, relic of a vanished farmhouse kitchen.

Many enthusiasts today buy up these rows of cottages and 'convert' them to houses. If they will study their purchases, they may find that all they have to do is to 'de-convert' their cottage row back to its original form as a farmhouse. (Fig. 16c).

The single-span is an essential feature of the planning system of the smaller English house until the eighteenth century. The old rooms go right across the house from side to side and are entered one from the other. During the mutilations following upon enclosures, some of the larger rooms were often divided into two down the middle so that each half had a window. It is nowadays quite easy to restore the original arrangement—though modern usage will generally require the provision of a corridor along one side so that the old room never gets back its original lighting.

Another—more glorious—fate to which the farmhouse whose owner was ruined by the Enclosure Acts might descend was for it to become an alehouse; many a farmhouse kitchen, as an alehouse kitchen, continued to dispense hospitality to the local rustics. Very many country pubs have their origins in this simple form of conversion.

Where farmhouses were set along a village street, some of their parlours became village shops. Look above the nineteenth-century shop fronts and again you will see the great chimney-stacks of other days (7).

So the farmhouse decayed and went to swell the ranks of the cottage homes which were at long last beginning to replace the peasant hovels of mediaeval times. With these conversions England bade farewell to the last of the rustic building-styles and prepared to become submerged in sophistication and smothered by stylistic Architecture devised by scholars and pedants.

For the time being, however, pseudo-rusticity was joyously established. Grottoes, sham ruins, follies, had long been popular (Marie Antoinette had fancied herself as a milkmaid!) During the Regency there was even a fashion for building lodges and suchlike unimportant structures of rounded logs with the bark still on them. Despite its complete irresponsibility, the period of the Regency must surely be the most delightful adventure in all the story of English architecture. Even its Gothicism was so naïve and unsophisticated—one has to admit that there was no direct copyism—only enthusiastic attempts to restore the *romance* of mediaeval masonry into life through the skill of the plasterer. All ordinance was deliberately defied—whether Classic or Gothic the designers were determined to keep everything light and gay, slender and soaring. A firm rejection of all solidity and pomposity . . . as unregenerate as the way of life of the Regent himself.

Glazing bars of windows engaged in further slimming so as to produce the daintiest pattern of tracery against the glass. The heavy Renaissance mouldings of the Georgian fireplaces were replaced by far lighter designs, incorporating motifs copied from the gayer forms of Classical Roman decoration.

The graceful designs of cast-iron interiors assisted in making the Regency fireplace a feature of considerable charm.

The old Classical architrave moulding using round internal door openings, small fireplace openings, inside windows, and so forth, was often abandoned in favour of the 'reeded' architrave with 'mitre blocks'—usually ornamented with a small turned patera—at the angles instead of the usual mitre. The reeded moulding also appears on chair-rails and is applied to lighten the surfaces of broad timbers in large windows and so forth.

Panelling practically disappeared, except where required for some romantic effect connected with mediaevalism. The 'Gothick' top appears on many panels, including those of doors, where this type of romanticism was sought in the design. Plaster wall surfaces began to be covered with wallpaper, a new material discovered in use in China.

With the coming of the Industrial Era, iron was bound to attract the attention of the house-builder. Its great beams were not used in small houses, but cast-iron posts were a delightful innovation in Regency verandas. These, once roofed with zinc, were now being covered with iron, either in flat sheets or in its corrugated form. This last, so much stronger than the flat sheet, became very popular for roofing such minor excrescences as rustic porches. Our colonial architecture may be said to have been founded on corrugated iron—in Australia, for instance, it still remains the standard form of roof covering.

The colonial empire was easily persuaded to add its contribution in the form of the bungalow type of villa and its outstanding feature, the veranda. Retired colonial administrators were little loth to raise their nostalgic verandas along the southern coasts of England. Supported by the slender posts —Classical or Gothic—of the Regency iron-founders, the daintiness of the English villa style of architecture was thereby greatly augmented.

For the country mansion, too, was dying out. It was in reality a relic of feudalism, often a white elephant requiring a mediaeval staff to keep it going. The villa was now the mode.

The villa, in origin a small country house, was becoming a feature of the suburbs. At first detached, with a central doorway and, perhaps, flanking bay windows, it could also be met with in the semi-detached style of the early Georgian cottages. As the suburbs of the larger cities expanded, villas merged into long ranges of two-storied houses, raised by speculative builders, and displaying whatever architectural treatment happened to be the current vogue. The 'double-fronted' plan, with the central entrance flanked by parlours, was less common than the 'single-fronted'—the original form of the seventeenth-century town house and that which developed into the 'universal plan' of the present century. This may now be met with in detached, semi-detached, or terrace form; it has the lateral entrance with the stair immediately inside it and the kitchen with bathroom over behind this, leaving two living-rooms with two bedrooms over for the main accommodation.

The beginning of the nineteenth century produced many charming urban 'terraces' of simple form, for occupation by clerical workers of simple means but large families. The compositions were of the utmost simplicity, with just the single windows lighting each floor and the dignified little doorway with its fanlight over. These little houses, now called 'cottages', are greatly sought after by the impoverished, maidless town-dweller of today.

After the pompous palatial treatments of eighteenth-century terraces, a lighter hand may generally be detected at work on urban house fronts. But the trend towards impeccable Classicism had been getting a foothold everywhere, and by the end of the Regency it had become firmly established.

The industrialism against which the frivolities of the Regency had provided an escape, strode relentlessly ahead as the clanking monsters of the railway tracks scared away the graceful phaetons and flying rigs of the Corinthians. Diehard romantics saw to it that the ghost of mediaeval England was not entirely exorcized, but for the time being they had to fight a rearguard action against the Classicists whose stern Doric seemed better suited to industrialist taste.

The middle third of the century was the heyday of heavy plaster Classicism in house-fronts. The rectory rebuilt for the Victorian paterfamilias is a good example of the style of the period.

Window treatment of the period can always be clearly detected. A model of Classical Athens, it displays the complete 'aedicule' treatment with the addition of a moulded sill supported by curled console brackets. The entrance doorway is probably covered with a solemn porch, usually in the Doric. The console bracket becomes a plague at this time. It appears beside doorways. Pairs of ghastly caricatures of the magnificent 'modillions' of Classical and Renaissance days cluster beneath extravagantly wide eaves. A somewhat meaner edition of the Georgian oriel appears during the Classical Revival era; of slight projection, it has severely plain fenestration.

The wrought ironwork of balustrades, poems of fans and spider webs during the Regency era, are replaced by tedious repetitions of cast-iron motifs usually based on the Classical acanthus.

The eighteen-thirties suffered under the serious-minded spirit of Reform. Amongst the items affected seems to have been Regency architecture—it was almost as though it no longer had the heart to multiply its cheerful pleasantries. Certainly the houses of the thirties, with their plain brick semi-circular arches and iron-barred casement windows, seem more in tune with the theme of contemporary workshop and factory.

The next decade—that of the railways—produced a sort of standardized type of house which might be termed 'Industrial Georgian'. Its square plan was focused on a central staircase hall, there were very plain elevations displaying sash windows glazed with large panes of sheet glass, and a front door-case in austere Doric with perhaps a simple porch.

A very noticeable feature of nineteenth-century houses is the lowering of the roof-pitch, hitherto nearly always more than forty-five degrees to the horizontal. Fifty to fifty-five degrees had been the normal pitch until the introduction of Welsh slates at the end of the eighteenth century. This close-fitting material enables a roof to be pitched as low as thirty degrees; a blessing to Classical-minded house-builders who hated to expose high-pitched roofs to the public view.

The distribution of this useful if not entirely attractive roofing material was achieved through the medium of the Georgian canal system. How pleasant it is today to encounter some memorial of that gracious era when our countryside was passing from the eighteenth century into the nineteenth. The wayside toll house thrusting its front into the turnpike road and windowed to scan both ways along it—the sturdy iron pump for village water supply or for laying the deep dust of the highway. And those once-busy canals which carried wheat, coal, and building materials across the countryside. Their beautifully-shaped bridges remain in scores. Weed-grown or dry, in ruined locks the great gates hang—immovable and seemingly indestructible—relics of the smooth and silent transport which preceded the rush and noise and fury of the Great Industrial Age.

After about 1810, gasworks had begun to rise beside the canals where these passed by country towns. Thereafter houses began to be designed with very lofty rooms in order to prevent the blackening of their ceilings and the asphyxiation of their occupants by the fumes from defective gas lighting. The mark of the 'gasolier' (dreadful successor of the chandelier) may be seen in the plaster 'roses' of Classical acanthus sprawling in the centres of the ceilings.

The Classicists were not allowed to flaunt their scholarship unchallenged. Romanticism may have for a time been smothered by the smoke from the tall chimneys, but the rural rectories sheltered plenty of clerical scholars who insisted that there was only one native English architecture—the Gothic.

The Gothic Revival was every bit as fanatical as the Classical movement. More serious than its sprightly predecessor of Regency days, the revivalists of the Mid-Victorian era revived everything to do with mediaevalism, including true masonry, and tried their utmost to reproduce buildings which were faithful copies of the work of mediaeval days.

'Half-timber work,' as the framing of houses in timber was called, was enthusiastically revived in the country areas, especially in those Home Counties whence the city magnate could travel to town by train. The timber used was sparse and of too small a scantling, the panels were filled with incredibly neat brickwork, laid herringbone, or plastered over with impeccably mediaeval ornament applied to the surface. Sometimes the whole gamut of tile-hanging was followed in order to omit nothing which might vary the elevations and make them interestingly mediaeval. Twisted chimney shafts became poems in moulded brick. Leaded lights in wrought-iron casements provided the correct fenestration; the sash window was very definitely excluded. Massive ledged doors, with 'thumb-latches' or primitive draw-bars for fastening, were part of the set-up for complete mediaevalism.

Much of the effort of the Gothic Revival went into the rebuilding of churches, and many mediaeval arts were revived to assist this. Stained glass received a fillip, and the ornamental floor-tile of mediaeval days reappeared once more. Domestic architects made use of such crafts to produce the maximum mediaeval effect in their 'Manors', 'Granges' (and even 'Abbeys' and 'Priories') the 'Minton' tile with its reds and browns and ochres became a ubiquitous feature of staircase halls of the period. Stained glass developed in the most extraordinary fashion, especially in half-glazed doors and in bathrooms.

Wallpaper spread throughout England in the Victorian era. The indefatigable William Morris—Gothic Revival craftsman *par excellence*—even devised mediaeval wallpapers which would not clash with the rest of the décor.

Throughout this strange escapist flirtation with treasures of other days, the normal development of English Renaissance architecture proceeded in somewhat dreary fashion. Windows, however, underwent a series of interesting modifications during the century. By Regency days, the glazing bars had become so slender that they could even be bent into 'Gothick' forms at the heads of the panes—a device which produced many charming features. At the same period the proportions of ordinary rectangular panes moved still farther away from the original almost square shapes—a square and a half or so is the pleasant Regency proportion (20).

The town house of the period often had the front windows of its fine first-floor rooms—the *piano nobile* of the Renaissance —carried down to the floor as 'french windows' and provided with balconies overlooking the street. The windows of these lofty rooms thus became very tall in relation to their widths, necessitating revision of the pane proportions to suit. The window of the middle of the first half of the nineteenth century has panes twice, or even two and a half times, as high as they are wide. Country houses of the period, which had no *piano nobile* but the normal ground floor living-rooms, had similar lofty windows reaching to the ground, through which the owner might step to reach his garden or park.

23. The Georgian house of the late eighteenth century represents the climax of English domestic architecture. The above example, at Blackheath in Kent, illustrates most of the well-known features of the style: the neat dormers, the fine Renaissance cornice, the tall sash windows with their glazing bars, the door-hood with its fanlight beneath it.

24. This stretch of the river front at Godmanchester in Huntingdonshire displays the two main types of small house contrasted. On the left are two single-span 'long' houses, each with its central stack; the finer house has a jettied-out chamber at its upper end. Both have been divided up into cottages and shops. To the right of them are two double-span 'square' houses of eighteenth-century date with gable chimneys; that on the extreme right has a mansard roof.

The Georgian window could play no part at all in the ordinance of the Gothic Revival House where the leaded light was the inflexible rule. Nor could it be accepted by the Classical Revivalists as providing a suitable form of fenestration for a Greek temple. The latter party was seriously incommoded by this problem. Early in the nineteenth century, by which period it had been found possible to make fairly large sheets of glass, the joiners invented the 'bordered' window which had as big a sheet as possible in the middle, surrounded by the slender glazing bars of the period, and a narrow border of strips of glass divided by short lengths of bar. Glazed and half-glazed doors were made and glazed in this pattern (it is to be regretted that the stained glass experts were so often let loose on the result!).

By the second quarter of the century the manufacturers had invented plate glass which could be rolled in large thick pieces requiring neither lead calms nor glazing bars. The Classical Revival windows could thus retain their box frames (they also had to retain, unfortunately, the 'meeting rails' of the sashes) but otherwise the simple opening of the temple window was left unmarred.

The 'Crystal Palace', designed at the middle of the century to house the Great Exhibition, popularized its curious technique of glass set in frames of cast iron, eventually producing as by-product a rash of 'conservatories' which clung in exotic fashion to many a fine old house as well as to contemporary Victorian villas.

Such vagaries of construction, added to occasional invasions by specimens of conventional styles culled from architectural history books, played considerable havoc with many a fine old house whose elevations have since had to be purged of these souvenirs of ephemeral taste.

After the middle of the century, metropolitan classicists were beginning to unbend a little; not only did they transfer their allegiance to the Italian Renaissance but even sidled a little nearer to the light-hearted Gothic by adopting the Venetian version of it. This started a general move amongst rural builders to add a little gaiety to their elevations by cambering lintels, adding key-blocks, or even providing complete semi-circular heads. The spirit behind all this was doubtless Renaissance, but during the last quarter of the century some curious effects were achieved. Yet the well-intentioned efforts of their builders have been at last rewarded, and all has now been absorbed within verdant settings to play its part in the charm and dignity of rural England.

The Victorian era produced large numbers of middle-class houses of considerable interest, carrying on the tradition of Georgian days by providing rectories, houses for the doctor and the attorney, each set in a pleasant garden which was a park in minuscule.

How enchanting they are, those mansions in miniature of England's halcyon days! Stand by the drive-gate and see how the walls rise from lawns dappled with the shadows from tall trees planted generations ago. Take away the car from the drive and hide it decently within the coach-house which—with stable, hayloft, and harness room—still stands in dutiful attendance. Try to retune your ear to that jingling clippety-clop . . . the song of the chariots of the past.

Yet, while the Victorian middle-class flourished, the real life of the countryside was dying. There was distant competition from the great fields of the colonies, while strange machines were destroying the livelihood of reaper and thresher. The country people were beginning to emigrate to those same colonies, or at least to the new factory in the town.

A century or so ago, our villages had twice their present population. But as the century wore on, the villages could be seen to be dying. Cob and thatch were silently slipping back again to the earth, to form low mounds barely discernible by the wayside. But stone and brick, and much of England's everlasting oak, remained.

The Battle of the Styles lost its savagery before the end of the century, but in domestic architecture it never died. The Gothic—whether he knows it or not—is deeply ingrained in the Englishman's soul. At the beginning of the present century a determined attempt was made to restore the Tudor timber-framed building in a careful fashion which paid proper attention to the original examples. The provincial architect of the first quarter of the century was still doing well with his 'Stockbroker's Gothic'. The 'half-timber' is in everyone's soul—we revel in it during our rural holidays and stick little bits of it on our suburban gables to this very day. We always shall.

We are not ashamed of our leaded lights. We cling firmly to the bay window, mediaeval in origin, its Georgian sashes replaced by hinged casements (filled, albeit, with sheet glass). Officialdom and the architectural schools may frown. They may build Neo-Georgian houses and force people to live in them (as they did after the first war) or strange soulless things in 'contemporary' style. But the speculative builder—who knows what his customers like—will always ignore his betters.

The English house has developed as a result of the achievements of the builders of each era in coping with new social problems and discovering new materials and methods. Other classes of building may have to conform to fashionable ideas in respect of taste; the man who wants a home is less concerned with what is and what is not *done*. If he accepts some popular *cliché*, he will agree to display it: that is as far as he can be made to go.

How much more contented a new house looks in a new suburb. And how unrewarding it is to try to introduce a new building into the bosom of the English countryside.

Designed by a sympathetic architect—yet on the most up-to-the-minute labour-saving plan incorporating every modern convenience framed within the gayest and glossiest decorative scheme conceivable—the whole achievement set in an expensively-wrought landscaped terrain of infinite variety . . .

It obtrudes, like a sore thumb, above its immaculate lawns and paths, while infant trees strive frantically to do their utmost towards tempering its startling immaturity.

(In less than a century, of course, after two or three generations have bestowed upon it the imprint of their several personalities, it will have become an accredited local inhabitant.)

The old houses of the countryside have long ago outgrown the pains of novelty. Their walls may have been neglected, their roofs in need of attention, their decorations renewal. They may from time to time have sprouted uncongenial excrescences to disturb their ancient dignity.

But their setting is assured—their patina genuine . . .

And what tales they have to tell!

147

Postscript

It must not be supposed that the foregoing chapters offer more than a general outline of the way in which the smaller English house developed through the centuries. What has been done has been to suggest the situation at each period and the attitude of the contemporary house-builder towards this. Reactions were far from being identical—for example the latter part of the seventeenth century and onwards saw different approaches to the problem of the obstructive central chimney-stack and various methods of augmenting the accommodation of the two principal variants of the standard plan of the period.

It is, however, by appreciating the underlying motives governing the attitude towards the house-plan at each era which enables one to attempt the unravelling of the history of some old building, a fascinating occupation especially for anyone fortunate to be living in some ancient English home.

Let us, for example, try to reconstruct in imagination the architectural history of a small fourteenth-century timber manor house of which the shell has survived to the present day. Visualize the simple barn-like structure about twenty-four feet wide set out in four bays of about sixteen feet each, each bay indicated by a timber frame crossing the building from side to side, five of them in all including the gable ends. The centre one may perhaps have been a wooden arch of 'cruck' form or built up in more sophisticated fashion to form a fine architectural feature; the remaining bay divisions would be represented by eight sturdy posts. Three bays would be the hall of the manor house itself, the other one divided into pantry and buttery by a cross partition and a central one. In the centre of the three

Postscript

remaining bays would be the wide fire-hearth, above this the dais; at the lower end of the hall next the cross partition would be the main entrance doorway. Above the two storerooms would be the bedchamber on its solar floor reached by a steep wooden stair or ladder. The roof would be of pairs of heavy rafters laid flat on their sides without any ridge piece, each pair of rafters joined together near the apex by a wooden collar.

A century and a half later, say after the end of the Wars of the Roses, the owner of our manor house might have separated the dais bay of the hall from the hall itself with another cross partition to form a parlour with a fine bedchamber above it, the solar timbers being projected over the side walls of the hall as 'jetties' carrying the gable ends of a new cross roof provided to give more headroom to the chamber. The open firehearth might have been moved to the centre of the curtailed hall or even abandoned altogether and a proper stone fireplace built against one of the side walls and ending in a chimney. The old solar floor over the storerooms might have been relaid with jetties, gables and a new cross roof to match that at the upper end of the hall. Thus the front of the house would now show a two-bay hall flanked by two-storied end bays each finished with a gable (cf. Fig. 6a). The hall might by this time have been dignified by the addition of an entrance porch.

A century later, perhaps during the reign of James I, we should probably see a massive brick chimney-stack rising up through the roof at the upper end of the hall, having in it fireplaces for hall and parlour on the ground floor and similar fireplaces on the upper floor to serve the great chamber and another chamber provided over the hall by inserting a floor. In the thickness of the base of this great chimney-stack, and between it and an outer wall, would be sited the new staircase winding round a central newel post. The old storerooms would probably have been knocked into a single room, the second-best or dining parlour. The windows would all have been enlarged, properly framed-up in good joinery with mullions, and filled with leaded glazing.

Yet another century passes and we find many changes in the appearance of the old building. Perhaps the ends of the old timber jetties have been picked up by ground floor brick walls, and the parlours thus extended by two or three feet. Perhaps

150

the second parlour has been provided with a chimney-stack in the end wall, so that the parlour and its chamber above may be heated.

By Georgian days the lower half-bay at the end of the hall might have been partitioned off to form a staircase hall with a 'dog-leg' staircase in it (cf. Fig. 16a), the old wooden spiral next the great chimney being ripped out and turned into a couple of cupboards. During this Georgian era all the old windows would be enlarged and provided with the new sash frames with wooden glazing bars instead of leaded lights. The old porch would go and be replaced by a doorcase of Renaissance style. Such portions of the old timber frame as may still remain visible externally might be covered with clapboarding, tile hanging, or lath and plaster. External woodwork would be painted white. The old fireplaces will be partly bricked up and fitted with iron grates, and embellished with Renaissance-type surrounds in moulded wood. Perhaps by Regency days we may see queer Gothic forms appearing in the ornamentation of doorways, windows and fireplaces.

Then with the nineteenth century we may see the house fallen on bad times and divided up to form a row of cottages. The centre portion with the great stack and the main stair might be left intact, or perhaps divided into two with a partition (cf. Fig. 16c); the end bays with the parlours and chambers over will be closed off from it and provided with their own entrance doorways and steep narrow staircases. Possibly if the house is now in a village street one of the cottages may become a shop and have its parlour window enlarged for display.

As we explore old houses we can generally trace back their history. We can see where the Elizabethan spiral stair once wound beside the great chimney-stack. We can detect on the undersides of old flat floor joists the grooves which indicate a vanished jetty. We can find old doorways, old windows. Up where the water tanks gurgle we may discover the centuries-old timbers of a mediaeval roof. And here and there, built up in brick walling or buried behind lath and plaster, we may still find the great posts of a house-frame first raised to the order of a man who went to war in plate-armour.

151

Glossary

———————— ✹ ————————

aedicule	form of frame round door or window based on miniature of end of Classical building or portico
architrave	lower member of Classical entablature (qv) also carried round door or window opening as frame
balloon frame	current engineering term for building-frame passing through more than one storey (12)
baluster	miniature ornamental column supporting handrail of balustrade
barge board	sloping board covering ends of roof timbers at verge (qv)
bay	longitudinal unit of building plan or elevation
bay-window	projecting three-sided window
binder	see 'girder'
bond	system of interlocking bricks or stones to avoid weakness through 'straight joints' (14)
bow-window	window projecting in a shallow arc
brace	short timber set obliquely to stiffen frame by introducing triangulation (12)
brattice	mediaeval boarded partition (also stockade)
calm	grooved lead strip for holding glass 'quarries' (qv) in leaded glazing (pron. 'came')
caracole	stair climbing from floor to floor in a semi-circle of steep steps[1]
casement	window opening on hinges
chair-rail	wooden rail set about three feet above floor of room to prevent damage to wall plaster by chair-backs
chamber	room on an upper floor

[1] In Spain the word *caracol*, meaning snail, is used for all spiral stairs.

153

Glossary

chamfer	a bevelled edge
chevron	see 'couple'
clapboard	see 'weatherboard'
cob	primitive concrete made of mud bound together with chopped straw
cockspur	ornamental fastener to old iron casement
collar	short length of timber tying together pair of rafters near apex
console bracket	S-shaped bracket, usually carved, supporting Renaissance door-hood
corbel	strong stone bracket
cornice	crowning member of Classical entablature (qv) also used as a finish to a wall-top (23) and below internal ceilings
couple	chevron; pair of rafters joined at apex by tie
cove	broad concave moulding
cruck	pair of large curved timbers carrying ridge of building direct from ground
dado-rail	see 'chair-rail'
dog-leg stair	stair formed of two flights joined by half-landing; 'pair of stairs'
dormer	small window set in roof timbering (16)
dragon beam	beam set in angle of jettied-out floor to assist joists in turning angle of building and carried by teazle-post (qv)
dressings	worked stone or brick surrounds to openings, also quoins and other features requiring special care
dripstone	projecting moulding over door or window used for diverting rainwater away from opening (see 'label')
eaves	projection of roof over wall-face
entablature	Classical horizontal feature joining tops of columns or crowning wall-face, comprises architrave, frieze and cornice
fanlight	small window, originally semicircular, set in head of door opening (23)
field-stone	see 'rubble'
freestone	stone capable of being dressed with tools
frieze	intermediate unmoulded component of Classi-

154

Glossary

	cal entablature (qv) also upper part of interior walling next ceiling
gable	end of building showing roof pitch
girder	beam passing between main posts of building
half-timber	modern term to describe timber-framed building
header	brick laid at right-angles to wall-face (14)
hip	roof-slope carried round angle of building
hipped end	end of building with roof-slope carried round to cross it
hip rafter	rafter supporting hip
housing	inserting one timber into another
jack rafter	short length of rafter resting against hip rafter
jetty	timber floor projecting over lower storey and carrying storey over (1)
joist	timber actually carrying floor boarding or ceiling plaster
king-post	central vertical member of roof 'truss' (qv)
label	square form of dripstone (qv)
lacing course	course or courses of masonry or brickwork set in flint or rubble walling in layers to strengthen it
light	unit of glazed window
mansard	roof constructed in two pitches, the steep lower portion acting as walls to attic storey (24)
modillion	S-shaped bracket supporting overhanging cornice
moulding	running ornament formed on surface or edge of stone, wood, plaster etc. by cutting or casting continuous lines of alternate swellings and hollows.
mullion	vertical member of wood or stone separating the lights of a window (15)
newel	vertical timber post supporting stair or balustrade
newel-stair	spiral stair revolving round newel
nogging	filling between timbering of house-frame
oriel	window projecting from upper floor or supported on bracket

155

Glossary

outshot	addition covered by a lean-to roof
parlour	ground-floor living-room
pediment	Classical feature comprising low-pitched gable ornamented by cornice moulding
piano nobile	upper floor containing principal apartments
pilaster	flat half-column attached to wall
plate	horizontal timber set on wall to carry joists or rafters; wall-plate
purlin	longitudinal timber supported by trusses (qv) gable walls etc. and carrying rafters
quarry	diamond-shaped pane of glass
queen-post	one of a pair of small posts forming part of a roof-truss (cf 'king-post')
quoin	angle of a building, or stones, bricks etc. forming it
rafter	sloping timbers to which roof covering is attached
reveal	side of opening through wall
ridge	line of meeting of roof-slopes at apex; small timber carrying this
rubble	stone gathered from fields or salvaged from old buildings and laid without dressing by tools (18)
rusticated quoins	those which project in front of the wall-face instead of being flush with it
sash	sliding wooden window, later used to denote any movable wooden window
shingle	long wooden tile for roof covering
sill	horizontal timber carrying vertical ones, foundation timber of framed house, lower timber of door or window frame
solar	mediaeval upper floor (pron. 'soller')
spandrel	approximately triangular space left between curve of arch or sloping timber and lines formed by adjacent horizontals and verticals
spur	short screen projecting inside external door of mediaeval apartment
stop	junction of moulding (qv) and unmoulded section of feature
stretcher	brick laid parallel to wall-face (14)

156

Glossary

string	sloping timber carrying steps of a staircase
string-course	horizontal projection passing across wall-face
stud	vertical timbers forming timber frame or framed partition
summer	heavy beam carrying wall or floor above (Fr. *sommier*—pack-horse)
teazle-post	post formed out of timber set butt-uppermost and with upper end left thickened-out to provide room for morticing lateral timbers (1)
tie-beam	heavy beam tying opposite walls together; foundation member of roof 'truss' (qv)
transom	horizontal member separating lights of tall window
trimming	framing opening formed in joists or rafters to accommodate stairs, dormer windows etc.
truss	strongly-framed triangular feature crossing building at bay interval and carrying ridge and purlins of roof
Venetian window	three-light window having centre light twice width of lateral ones and usually semi-circular-headed
verge	edge of roof at gable end
voussoir	wedge-shaped stone or brick used in arch
wall-plate	horizontal timber set on top of wall to carry feet of rafters
wattle	woven willow-wands used as foundation for plaster of cob or, later, lime
weatherboard	board used for external sheathing of timber frames and set overlapping like the strakes used in boat-building, clapboard
wind-brace	arched timber set in pairs, strutting purlins from trusses to prevent longitudinal collapse of roof from pressure on gable end

157

Index

See also Glossary, *pages 153 to 157, for indications of architectural features illustrated in the Plates.*

'Abbeys', 'granges', etc. (nineteenth century), 144
Abbots' houses, twelfth century, 30; private halls, 38
Adam ceilings, 82
Aedicule, *see* Door case; Georgian, 119–20; Victorian, 141–2
Alberti, 65
Aldhelm, St., churches of, 23
Alehouses, 139
Almshouses, 121
Anglo-Saxon characteristics, 21, 22; Byzantine influences affecting, 23, 26, 27, 38, 40
Arabesque ornament (door case), 81
Arabic numerals, introduction of, 56, 83, 93
Arched crucks, 90
Architects: seventeenth century builders as, 100; numbers, by late seventeenth century, 111; in nineteenth century 'Battle of the Styles', 136
Attics: origin of, 71; lighting of, 72; as hidey-holes, 83; seventeenth century, 87; lead- and slate- improvements to, 112
Auger, first use of, 21

Back yards, early, 60
Baking ovens, seventeenth-century farmhouse, 92
Balconies, Victorian, 144
Balloon frames, early, 69; later, 85, 86, Pl. 12 (Cropthorne)

Baluster and balustrade, introduction of, 73, 81; Elizabethan, Jacobean, 81; Commonwealth, 103; Regency and after, 142
Barbon (Barebones), first town estate developer, 102
Barge-boards, 122; of nineteenth century Gothic revival, 135, 136
Barn, byre, as part of house, 91
Bath stone, 23, 124, 127
'Bay system', mediaeval, 103; bay windows, 40; Georgian reappearance of, 119; *see* Windows
Becket, Thomas, murder of, 92
Beckford, William, builder of Fonthill Abbey, 135
Bedford, Dukes of, in townhouse development, 102
Bed-testers, 61
Benedictines, 23, 30
'Bird's-nest' grates, 129
Bishops' houses: twelfth century, adjoining cathedrals, 30; 'great chambers', 33; halls, 31, 32; palaces, as cream of mediaeval building, 33, 35, 38
Black Death, effect of on window siting, 89
Block-course (parapet), Georgian, 120
'Bolection' moulding, fireplace frame, Georgian, 128
Bosporthprennis, near Penzance, dome-roofed house at, 20
Bow window, Georgian, 119; *see* Windows

Index

'Bowers' (parlours), 40
Box frames of windows, 106–7, 129; behind outer brickwork, 119; setting back of, as fire precaution, 119
Bracketed, door hoods, 122, 138
Brattiang, 45; for wainscot, 82; on board walls, 60, 70
Bricks: early East Anglian, 68; early, for fireplaces, chimney-stacks, 68–9, 73–4; for ground storey, with Tudor upper storey, 103; great seventeenth-century influence of, 100; earliest bricklayers and brickyards, 69, 80, 85, 100; Georgian, 116; bond, 85–6; herringbone, 143; quoins, 87; stucco-covered, 117, 118; wagon cartage of, 93; brick arch replacing oak lintel, 100; 'lacing course', 101
Building contracts, earliest, 24
Building metrology (old houses), 25
Bungalow 26, 27, 140
Butteries, drink-stores of early 'halls', 31, 54
Buttresses (wall and pinnacle), 37, 39
Byzantine influences, 23, 26, 27, 38, 40

Calms, of windows, 63, 106
Canal transport, 142–3
Caracoles, 41–2, 60, 75, 79; early seventeenth century, Fig. 13 (p. 104) eighteenth century, 124
Casements, Tudor, 63; Georgian revival of, 132; see Windows
Ceilings: carved, of parlour, 41; moulded edges of joists, 48; patterns (floor timbers), 69–70; plastering of Tudor beamed, 81; ornamented plaster, 82; see Cornice
Cellar as insulator, seventeenth century, 130

Central stack, 97
Central staircase hall, preceding corridor, 99–100
Chair-rail, introduced, 131
Chalk walling, 47
Chamber-parlour basic system, 41
'Chambers of estate', 54, 112
Chamfered ceiling mouldings, 48
Chapels, of King John's houses, 28
Chevrons, 37
Chimney: Tudor, 55; late Tudor opulence of, 62–3; chimney-stacks; two-storeyed, 62; example of late sixteenth century, Pl. 2 (Houghton); early seventeenth century, Pl. 7 (Grantchester); invention of internal, 73; Elizabethan and Jacobean, 73, 74, 75; incorporated with gable, seventeenth century, 89; central, with double-span plan, 97; later seventeenth century, 79, 92; early eighteenth century, 112–14, 130; Georgian, 98, 120, 121, Fig. 12 (p. 98)
Chimney canopies on corbels, fifteenth century disappearance of, 63
Chimney clusters (Elizabethan and Jacobean), 74, 81
Chimney pieces, seventeenth century 'Great Parlour', 99
Chimney shafts, twisted, mid-Victorian Gothic, 143
Chisel, first use of, 21
Churches: early, 26; as monopolizers of masoncraft, 23–4; mid-Victorian, 144
Chysauster, Cornwall, homes round circular courtyards, 20
Cistercian abbots' houses, 30
Civil War, 92–3, 114, 134
Clapboarding, Georgian, 115
Classical Revival, nineteenth century, 141–2
Clay: as wall core, 23; as thatching, 18; tiles, roofing, 76, 89

159

Clerical private houses, 30
'Cloth-yard', mediaeval, 25
Clustered chimney shafts, 74, 81
Coach houses, 125-6
Coal as new fuel, 91, 128-9
Cob, cob and wattle, 36-7, 46-7, 124; cob walls, 13
Cockspur casement fastenings, 63, 129
Collars (rafters, chevrons), 37, 51
'Colonial house', 115
Concrete, 36, 137
Conservatories, 145
'Conversion' as modern device, 91
Cord, as firewood measure, 25; cordwood, 74
Cornice: Elizabethan, over doorways and windows, 78; Georgian, joinery or plaster (wall-and-ceiling), 132
Cotswold: stone building, 78-9, 85, 107, 108; Yorkshire echoes, eighteenth century, 124; many-gabled Jacobean, 72; chamber gable, Pl. 15 (Stanton). *See* Cruciform
Cottages: mediaeval, 36; surviving mediaeval, 42; origin of present-day, 58; Georgian, 126, 128; cottage rows, Georgian, 137, 138, Pls. 16, 17, Fig. 16c (p. 123); rubble-stone Cornish, Pl. 18 (Boscastle); nineteenth century 'romantic', Pl. 22; terrace, 141
'Couples' (rafters with collar), 50, 51; disappearance of, 71-2
'Coves' of Tudor buildings, 50; *see* Dentil course
Cross-beams, Jacobean, 69, 70
Cruciform windows, seventeenth century, 87; boxed sashes replace, 106-7; persisting in stone belt, 108, 109
Crucks (roof-tree timbers, supports), 35-6, 45, 50, 90, Pl. 3 (Lacock)
Crusades, 27-8

Crystal Palace, 145
Curved braces, late sixteenth century, 67

Dado-rail, 131
Dais, of early 'hall', 32, 33, 38
Date over entries to houses, 83
Decimal and duodecimal systems, 26
'Dentil course', replacing coving, 78
Dining-room, origin of, 68
Dissolution of the Monasteries, architectural developments following, 30, 60-3, 93, 97, 114
Dog-leg stairs, 102-3, 114
Domed roofs (field-stone), 20
Domestic architecture, classifications of, 14, 37
Doors: doorways in cob houses, 47; Anglo-Saxon plank, 22; Tudor, 63, 77; seventeenth century long-house, 86; nineteenth century glazed and half-glazed, 145; modern sheath, 131; door-cases, Renaissance, 81; door-frames, 131; Elizabethan joinery, 83; ledged, mid-Victorian, 144; door-hoods, 106, 122-4; lock-rail introduced, 131
Dormer windows, 13, 72, 107, Pl. 16
Double-parlour houses, 97, Pl. 10 (Charmouth)
Double window, shuttered, King John's houses, 28
'Dragon' beam, origin of, 52
Drains as 'secret passages', 42
Draw-bars: Tudor, 63; of Gothic revival, 143
Drawing-rooms, 130
Dutch gables (East Anglia), 89

Eaved-all-round thatch, 76
Eaves and cornice-capped elevations, gables replaced by, 101
Edgehill, Battle of, 25

Index

Edinburgh, 15, 69
Elizabethan and Jacobean standard planning, 65–83; E-shaped mansion, 66; entrance doorways, 77; many-roomed houses 71; persistent tradition in Cotswolds, 108, 109; drabness after passing of, 92–3
Enclosure Acts, Georgian, 137–8, 139
End elevations, gable-ends replaced by, 99
End stacks, as Georgian additions, 121
'English bond', Elizabethan origins of, 85–6
Entrance doorways: Elizabethan, 77; seventeenth century developments, 106; Georgian, 120, 122

Fanlights, 103, 141; with door hood, Pl. 23 (Blackheath)
Farmhouses (or yeomen's houses), origin of, 58; as copy, 90; brick replacing framed walling, 86; late Tudor, 66–7; brick chimney-stacks of (Tudor), 69; standard Elizabethan, Jacobean, 73–6, Fig. 7 (p. 75); humbler, Fig. 13 (p. 100); rubble-stone, Fig. 9 (p. 80); standard late sixteenth century converted, Pl. 4 (Aldbury); an eighteenth century conversion, Pl. 8 (Gt. Bardfield); of seventeenth century, 79, 80, 91, 92, 108, Fig. 9 (p. 80), Fig. 13 (p. 100); parlourless seventeenth century, Pl. 9 (Salford Priors); winter parlours of, Fig. 8c (p. 77), Pl. 10 (Charmouth); development of manorial type, seventeenth and eighteenth century, 98, Fig. 11 (p. 95); early eighteenth century with central stack, 112; later

changes, 131; Georgian, 137; becoming alehouse, 137; becoming cottage rows, 137, 138; Fig. 16 (p. 123), Pls. 16 (Broadway), 17 (Wherwell); parlours of, as village shops, 139; single-parlour, 122, Pl. 5 (Eling), Pl. 6 (Somersby), Pl. 12 (Cropthorne)
Farnham (Surrey), Bishop's Palace, a twelfth-century survival in, 32
Feudal: hall, Fig. 1 (p. 24), Fig. 3 (p. 31); decline of system and Great Hall, 31 seq.
Field stone, 20; ragstone replacing, 23
'Fielded panels', Georgian, 131
Firebacks, Elizabethan, 74; seventeenth century, 91; coal and, 129
Firedogs, 74
Fireplaces: Tudor, 53, 54, 61, 62; Elizabethan, 74; later seventeenth century, 91–2; with seat and shelf recesses, 92; Georgian, 128; Regency, 139
'Flashings' of chimney stack, 97
'Flemish bond', 86
Flint: and chalk building, 101, 124; and freestone, 80, Pl. 14 (Broadchalke)
Floor joists: mediaeval, 48; Jacobean mid-span support of, 69–70
Follies, 139
Fonthill Abbey, 135
Foot, origin of measurement, 25
Fortified commercial centres, 58–59
Framed (timber) houses: Roman, 20, 21; Tudor, 56, 57; prefabrication of frames, 73
Freestone: early dressing of, 23; with flint, see Flint; see Cotswolds; various uses of, 36, 63, 124
Froissart, on humble cottages, 36

Gables: Anglo-Saxon absence of, 22–3; of early 'halls', 24, 30–1; gable ends: Tudor changes, 51, 52; with thatch, 76, 77; seventeenth century, 89; Georgian disappearance of, 120; Regency revival of, 136; 'gable-fork', 90; gable stack, eighteenth–nineteenth century, 62; gable stacks (pairs) replacing great stack, 113–14

Gablets: as garret improvers, 72; rustic use of, 72; developments, 118, Pl. 12 (Cropthorne); dormers replace, 107; Cotswolds pinnacled, 108, 109

'Garden wall bond', Pl. 14 (Broadchalke)

Gargoyles, use of, 96

Garret, origin of, 71, 72

Gasoliers, 143

Gaslighting, gasworks, 143

Gates, Georgian, 132–3

Gazebos, 125

Georgian developments, 111–33; house plan, 58, Fig. 12 (p 98); as modification of long house, 122, 127, 128, Fig. 16 (p. 123); late eighteenth century, Pl. 23 (Blackheath); cottages, 73, 95, Figs. 13, 14 (pp. 104, 113); inns, 102; windows, 107, 133, Pl. 8 (Great Bardfield), Pl. 23 (Blackheath); transition to Victorian Doric, 136–7

Girder (beam), Tudor, 52

Glazing bars, wooden (sash), 106, 107

Gothic, 38, 48; opponents of, 136; nineteenth-century revival, 135, 136, 143–4, Pl. 22 (New Forest); as reaction to Industrial Revolution, Pl. 21 (Winterbourne Came)

Grand Tour, 134

Great Halls, 31–5, 129, 130, *see* Halls

Great Parlour, ancestor of drawing-room, 99

Greek Orders, 136

Greensted Church, Essex, 46

Grizels, 117

Grottoes, 139

Ground-sill, as Anglo-Saxon innovation, 22

Gutters, 96–7; box, with parapet, Georgian, 120; valley, Fig. 11 (p. 95)

Half-timbering, three stages of, 46, 56, 57, 143, 146

Halls (upper-class homes), 30, 31, 32; as public assembly rooms, 33, 59; King John house added to, as mediaeval 'great house', 33; late mediaeval, 35; end of stone-built aisled (thirteenth century), 38; porched (fourteenth century), 39–40; with one or two storeys added, 38; lineage of timber, 46; developing into farmhouse kitchen, 54; modern use of term, 41; tiny, as chimney (sixteenth century), 55; hall-screen and minstrels' gallery, 82–3

'Headers', bricklayers' use of, 117

Hearths of early halls, 31

Heather: as fuel, 92; as thatch, 18

Henry II: castles, 27; fire precautions, 30

Henry VIII, meets Francis I in France, 65; timber building in reign of, 60–4

Hereford, Bishops' Hall, twelfth-century survival in, 32

Hidey-holes, 83

High Streets, origin of, 93

Hinges, eighteenth century, 132

Hipped roofs, eighteenth century, 122; of early double-span houses, 97, 98; 'hips' of thatched roofs, 76

Hobs, of Georgian high grates, 129

Index

Hooks and bands: door, 63, 83; window, 129

Houses, fifteenth and sixteenth century distribution of, 57–8

Hunting lodges, 96

Industrial age, 14, 128–9, 135, 140; see Gothic; 'Industrial Georgian, 142

Inn sign brackets, eighteenth century, 133

Inns: Tudor, 59; Georgian, 101

'Interior grates', 74

Internal: chimney-stack, 73; partitioning, mediaeval, 70; timbering, sheathing of, 82

Interlocking tiles, seventeenth century, 89

Iron: ironwork of Tudor mullioned windows, 63; straps, on intersecting beams, 70; of Elizabethan and Jacobean fireplaces, 74; hand-wrought casements, 86; seventeenth-century casements, 87; corrugated, 123, 140; cast-iron fireplace interiors, 128–9; wrought-iron, Georgian, 132; glazing bars (factory), Gothic revival, 136, Pl. 21; and Industrial Age, 140; cast-iron Regency veranda posts, 140; Regency use of corrugated, 140; pumps, 143

Islamic influence, 37, 40–1

'Jack' rafters, 76

Jacobean, 65 seq.; jettyless timber houses, 69, 70; James I 'stykkes to brykkes', 69

Jetties, jettying-out of storey, 49–50, 55, 58, 66–7, 69, 73; obliteration of, 103

John, see King John

Joinery, new eighteenth century timbers for, 114

Joinery cornice, Georgian, 132

Joint-pinning, Anglo-Saxon, 21

Joints: coded, Tudor half-timber, 56–7

Joists: softwood laid on edge, 105–6

Keep-towers, 27, 28

Key-blocks, 145

King John's houses, 28, 35, 38, 40, 50, 52; surviving, 30; as parts of twelfth-century royal palaces, 32–4

King-posts: Tudor, 51; Elizabethan, 71; and 'hip' rafters, 76; Georgian, 124

Kitchen-pantry, of early halls, 31; of Tudor inns, 59

Knee crucks, 90

L-plan, origin of, 127, Fig. 17 (p. 127); Georgian wing added, 127–8

Labels, 108, Pl. 14 (Broadchalke)

Labourers' cottages, eighteenth century, 125–6

'Lacing course', 101

Lath and plaster: as balloon-frame sheathing, 86; concealing softwood joists, 105–6, 116

Latrines, of King John's houses, 28

Lead: for roofing, after Dissolution, 61; for chimney gutters, 62; and central chimney-stack development, 97; for parapet gutters, 97; 'lead flats' (of double-span roofs), 98

Lead oxide, first use of as timber preservative, 114–15

Leaded glazed windows, 77, 87

'Ledgers' of doors, 63

Limestone burning (mortar), 23, 80

Limewash on rubblestone, 124–5. See Rubblestone

Lincoln, Jewish merchants' twelfth-century houses in, 29

Linenfold panel moulding, 82

Lock-rail, 131

'Lodges' (masons'), 96

Lodge and toll-house, Georgian, 121; Regency barked-log, 139

Index

'Lodgings': of fourteenth-century castles, 34; of cathedral canons, 34; for guests (Tudor), 62
Long gallery, Elizabethan, 99
Long houses, seventeenth century, 84–110; earliest, 76, 77; asymmetry as clue to age of, 121; decline of, 95; see Fig. 8 (p. 78); squaring up of, Fig. 15 (p. 116); Georgian modifications, Fig. 16 (p. 123); wings added to, 88, Fig. 10 (p. 88); single-span, Pl. 24 (Godmanchester)

'Magpie'-timbered houses, Midlands, 68
Manor houses: feudal, Fig. 3 (p. 31); mediaeval, Fig. 1 (p. 24); Tudor, 38–41, Fig. 5 (p. 39); possible evolution of fourteenth-century timber, 149–151; as first farmhouses, 58; and township, 57–8; Renaissance, Fig. 11 (p. 95)
Mansard roofs, 120, Pl. 24 (Godmanchester);
Market towns, development of, 58
Masonry technique, birth of, 19–23; masons released by Dissolution of Monasteries, 61–2
Mediaeval house, 17–42
Mensuration, mediaeval, 25
Merchants' houses, early, 58–9
Middle-class prosperity, 42, 44, 45
Minstrels' galleries, 83
Minton tiles, Victorian, 144
Moats, 46
Modillions, 142
Monasteries, 26, 30, 38, 61; attached to transepts, 30; as 'quarries', after Dissolution, 61
Morris, William, 144
Mortar, early, 23
Mortice and tenon, Anglo-Saxon, 21
Mosaic (tessellated) floors, 26

Moslem contacts, twelfth century, 27–8
Moxon's textbook for builders, 94
Mud-concrete, see Cob
Mud walling, 46, 47
Mullions, 38, 63, 77 (see Windows); central, of seventeenth century, 87; persisting in humbler buildings, 88, 124, 129; persisting in stone belt, 108; in North and West, 124
Multi-storey house, 71, 72

Napoleonic blockade, 137–8
Neo-Georgian style, post-War I, 137
Newels, 73, 75, 103
Newton, Sir Isaac, 94
Niches (from inside projection of stacks), 120
Nineteenth-century contribution, 134–48
'Nogging', 46, 55, 67, 117
Norman castle-keep towers, 27
Novels, influence of, 134–5

Oak: Tudor use of, 56, 60; 'oak beam' effect with softwood joists, 105–6; chimney beam (Elizabethan farmhouse), 74; as window timber, 77
Oriel windows: in jettied buildings, 50; Georgian, 119, 142
Outshot, 96, 100, 113, 122, 126, Fig. 15A (p. 116)
Oval huts, 21
Overdoor and entablature, 132
Overmantels, 74, 91

Paint, nineteenth-century coloured, 115
Panelling, see Linenfold, Wainscot; Georgian innovations, 131–2; Regency disappearance, 140; house-front, 117
Pantiles, 89
Pantry: as bread-store, 31; of bishops palace, 33

Parapetted: gables, 89; gutters, 96, 97

Pargetted panels, house-front, 117

Parlour: as store- and treasure-room, 40, 41; as bower, etc., 40, 91; as workshops, 121; parlourless seventeenth century house, one-parloured, two-parloured, 76 seq., Fig. 8

Parterres, perrons, etc., Georgian, 125

Peasants' Revolt, 44

Piano nobile, 26, 27, 28, 34, 99, 130, 144

Pinnacles with buttresses, 39

Pit-sawn timber, 21, 36, 37

Plague (Black Death), 15, 43–4

Plans and models, Tudor, 66

Plastering, 81–2, 117; concealing bad work, 106; ornamental Georgian and Regency, 120, 139, Pl. 23 (Blackheath); and classicism of mid-nineteenth century, 141

Plate glass, 145

Plough oxen: under hall roof, 24; role of, in mediaeval mensuration, 25

'Pole, furlong, acre', etc., 25

Porch: fourteenth-century hall, 39–40; Elizabethan porch-room, 83; Renaissance, 106; Cotswold, 108; trellis, Pl. 20 (Box Hill); nineteenth-century rustic, 140

Priests' houses, 33, Fig. 4 (p. 34)

Printing, 93

Pseudo-rusticity, nineteenth century, 139

Public buildings, origin of, 59

'Pulling down' of houses, origin of phrase, 57

Purlins: Tudor, 51; Elizabethan, 71, 72; of seventeenth century long-house roof, 87; Georgian, 124

'Quarries' (diamond-shaped Tudor panes), 63; panes replacing, 77, 106; of dormer windows, 107–8; in nineteenth-century Gothic, 136

Quarrying, 23, 124, 127

Queen-posts: Elizabethan, with collar, 71–2; Georgian, 124

Quoins, 87; brick, 101; stone, among brickwork, 116

Rafters: and thatch, 18, 19, 20, 21, 22; in stone-walled church roofs, 24; as royal gifts, 37; coupled, 50, 51; Elizabethan, Jacobean, 71, 72; 'jack' and 'hip', 76

Ragstone, 23

Railings, Georgian, 132–3

Railways, 141, 142

Raleigh, Sir Walter, 92

Rectory architecture, 141, 143

Red-brick, white woodwork, of Georgian house, 127, Pl. 23

'Red masons', 80, 85

Reed and straw thatch, 18

Reeded moulding, Regency use of, 140

Refectory, 33, 131

Regency, 129–31, 135, 139; sheathed softwood, 115; white houses, 117–18; 'Regency Gothic', Pl. 8 (great Gardfield); villa of, Pl. 20 (Box Hill); travellers of, 134–5; triptych windows, 133 (*and see* Windows)

Renaissance, 14, 65 seq., 102

Restoration, 94 seq., 107, 109

Ridge (roof), 24, 35

Roads (Georgian), 126, 127; see High Streets

Roman influences, 18, 20, 21, 26; Roman bricks for rubble wall angles, 23

Romsey, 30

Roofs: roof tree support, independently of rafters, 35–6; fourteenth-century lead-

Roofs—*cont.*
  sheeted, low-pitch, 39; village developments, 45; Tudor, 55, 60; great Tudor problem of, 50, 51; roof trusses, Tudor, 51; roof space as third storey, 71; Elizabethan and Jacobean changes, 70–2; new pitch, 76; eighteenth century long-house, 87; wide-span, 97–8; Georgian, 120, 124; mansard, 120; Regency corrugated iron, 140; nineteenth-century lowered pitch, 142
Royal palaces of twelfth century, 32–3
Royal Society, founding of, 94
Rubblestone, 13, 124, Pl. 11 (Selworthy)
Rural renaissance, 122–6

Salons, 129–30
Salt niche, in fireplace wall, 92
Salzman, L. F., *Building in England*, 22n
Sash window, late seventeenth century, 106; as Georgian feature, 118; *see* Windows
Sawyers, Anglo-Saxon, 21; *see* Pit-sawn
Scandinavian softwood, 105, 114
'Screens' of Tudor houses, 82; *see* Spurs
Secret rooms, 83
'Secret gutters', 98
'Secret passages', *see* Drains
Semi-basements, Georgian, 130
Semi-detached cottages, 126
Servants' accommodation, 71
Service area, service hatches (halls), 32
Sewage, waterborne, of monasteries, 61
Sham ruins, 139
Sheep, Tudor prosperity from, 44; *see* Wool
Sheet glass, 107, 142
Shingling, 117

'Ships' timbers' fallacy, 105
Shop fronts, 59, 77, 119
Shutters, Anglo-Saxon, 22
Single- and double-fronted villas, 141
Single- and double-parlours, *see* Parlours
Single-span, 95, 96, 138, 139
'Sixteen-foot pole', 25
Slates, *see* Welsh slates
Smiths' work, Georgian, 133
Softwood: imports, 105, 114; framing, 115–16; joists, 105–6. *See* Plastering
Solar (floor) of King John's houses, 28; stair to, 40
Spandrels of fireplaces, carvings on, 63
Spanish tiles, 89
Spinal beam, as floor support, 70–1, 104, 105
Spiral staircase, 79, Fig. 16A (p. 123), *see* Caracole; dog-leg ousting, 102, 103
Spurs (Tudor draught screens), 32, 82
Squaring of timbers, 21
Square houses, 109–10, 111 seq. Fig. 15 (p. 116), Pl. 24 (Godmanchester)
Squires, Georgian, parklands of, 125
Stabling, 59–60, 101
Stained glass, mid-Victorian, 144, 145
Stairs, staircases (*see also* Spiral): first step towards indoor, 40; Elizabethan timber, 42; ladder-like, of open hall, 67; of Elizabethan yeomen's houses, 67; of multi-storey houses, 72–3; of Cotswolds stone houses, 79; of long-gallery houses, 99; of Commonwealth, as triumph of joinery, 102; dog-leg, of terrace houses, 102, 103; Georgian, 113–14; eighteenth century enclosed, 124

Index

Standardized houses, seventeenth century onward, 65, 84 seq.

Steel building, 137

'Stockbrokers' Gothic', 146

Stone belt, 124, 127, Fig. 2 (p. 29). *See* Cotswolds; about twelfth century, 28 seq.; thirteenth century, 34; sixteenth century 67; Tudor oak and, 56; stone arcades replacing timber posts (halls), 31; stone solar, 28; stone wall as partition, first appearance of, 34–5

'Stops' of chamfered beams (Tudor), 49

Strap hinges, 132

Strawberry Hill, 135, 136

Street frontage, mediaeval, 101

String course, seventeenth-century feature, 86

Stuart and Revett ('Battle of the Styles'), 136

Stucco, 117

'Studs' of framed walls, 46, 47

'Sub rosa', 70

Summers (beams): Tudor, 52; at first floor level (Jacobean), 70; with slotted housings, 105; eighteenth-century changes, 113

'Sussex hips', 77, 117, Pl. 5 (Eling), Pl. 13 (Groombridge)

Surveyors, as architects, 63–4, 65–6, 67

Teazle posts, 66, 86, Pl. 1 (Lavenham)

Terrace houses, 102–3, 141

Tesseral, 20–1

Thatch: early bracken, turf, clay, wattle, 18, 19; Anglo-Saxon 'thatch-tile' (shingle), 22; developments, 76, 124; for cob walls, 47

Thirteenth-century town house, 29

Thorpe, John (Tudor surveyor), 66, 97

Three-storey small house, earliest, 71–2

Thumb-latches, 144

Tie-beams, 51, 71

Tile (clay) replacing thatch, 117

Tile-hanging, 117, P. 13 (Groom bridge)

Timber: framing, as early walling, 36; 'skyscrapers', mediaeval, 59; braced and pannelled, 67–9; of interior partitioning, 70–1; seventeenth-century framing with, 89–90; shortage of pre-Armada, 67, 85, 104, Pl. 4 (Aldbury), Pl. 12 (Cropthorne). *See* Tudor

Toll houses, 121, 126, 142

Town houses, slow development of, 28–30, 101 seq.

Tower, as porch development, 40

Transoms of windows, 77, 87

Transport, after Civil War, 93

Trellis work, 123, Pl. 20

'Trimmers', 76

'Triptych' windows, 119, 133

Tudor: yeomen, 43–64; principles of timber construction, 51–2

Turf thatch, 18, 19

'Turnpike Trusts', 126

Turret lights, Georgian staircase, 114

Twelfth-century town house, 28–29

Twelve-foot module, 25–6

Two-parlour houses, 71, 90, Fig. 8 (p. 78)

Union Jack, or ridge timber, 57

'Upper end' in new wing construction, 109

Upper floor: as monastic innovation, 26; separate entry to, 34

Vaulted ground floors, twelfth century and thirteenth century, 29–30

Venetian: Gothic, 145–6; window, 119, 133

Verandas, Regency, 140
'Verge' of gables, 89
Victorian building, 141 seq.;
  middle-classes houses, 146;
  rectories, 141
Vignola, 65, 81
Villas: replacing country namor,
  140; suburban, 140–1; semi-
  detached, 141; *see* Regency
Village, origin of, 45; Georgian,
  125; Victorian decline of, 146
Voussoirs, 108

Wainscot, 82
Walls, walling, 23; late mediae-
  val, 35, 36; concrete, 36; with
  timber framing, 36; structure
  of masonry, 36; buttressed, 37;
  crenellated, 39; of 'bratticing',
  45; framed, later, 46; cob and
  wattle, 46–7; *see also* Timber
Wall fireplaces, eleventh-century
  origin of, 62; types of, 53, 54,
  66, 68–9
Wall panelling, dado-rail and, 131
Wallpaper: Regency, 140; Victorian, 144
Walpole, Horace, 135
Wars of the Roses, 53
Watermills, S. England, 115
Wattle and daub, 18
Weatherboarding, 115
Welsh slates, roof pitch and, 142
White houses, late eighteenth
  century, 117; Georgian white
  paint, 115; watermills, 115
Wind braces, Tudor timber
  arches, 51
Wind-eyes, 47
Windows various aspects: arches
  of Tudor lights, 63; attitudes
  to, changing, 88–9; bay, 40,
  119, 130, 140, Pls. 8, 10, 13;
  Black Death and, 89; bordered
  (nineteenth century), 145;
  casement, 87, 129, 133, *see*
  Casements, Pls. 11, 13; Cruciform, 87, and *see* Cruciform;

former, 72, 107, Pl. 23; double-
  opening, central shaft, 38;
  Elizabethan wide, 78; factory-
  made glazing bars for, Pl. 21;
  fanlight, 103; French, 144;
  Georgian (various), 111, 118,
  119, 127, 130, 132, Pls. 8, 23;
  lighting dais, 40; mullioned,
  38, 63, 77, 87, 88, 124, 129;
  stone-belt retaining, 108; *see*
  Pls. 14, 15; mullioned, Gothic
  revival, 136; oak-barred, 47;
  oriel, 50, 119, Pl. 2; Georgian
  oriel, 119, 142; Palladian, 133;
  plate glass, 145; Regency, 133,
  139, 144, Pl. 20; Renaissance
  proportions, 87; sash, 106,–7
  118; squared timber framed,
  seventeenth century, 86; shop,
  77; traceried glass-filled, 35;
  triptych, 119, 133; Tudor
  manor-house, 38; Venetian,
  119, 133; Victorian Gothic,
  145; villa, 140; of wood, cob,
  wattle walls, 47; workshop, 18,
  121; wrought-iron casement,
  with leaded lights, 143
Wings in long-house restoration,
  109, Fig. 10 (p. 88)
Winter parlours, 68, 90, Fig. 8c
  (p. 78)
'Withdrawing room', 130
Wood-turning lathe, introduction
  of, 102
Wool trade, 44, 52, 55, 85
Wrights' (house carpenters')
  work, 21, 35, 36, 45; as main
  village contribution, 37
Wrought-iron: casements, 143;
  railings (Georgian), 132

Yeomen's houses, 43 seq., Fig. 6
  (p. 54)
Yorkshire eighteenth-century
  stone-houses, 124

Zinc-roofed verandas, 140
Zones (regional), 14–15